PRAISE FOR
LEADERSHIP TOOLKIT FOR ASIANS

"Jane has brought data-driven insights and her heart for coaching for as long as I've known her, and this book doesn't disappoint. Her extensive experience has created a powerful and compelling road map for developing leaders with influence. This toolkit brings deep subject matter expertise from her work with Asian leaders around the world, intercultural insights, and strategic thinking to build on her first book. This book is for anyone who seeks to lead inclusively."

—**DAVID A. THOMAS, PhD,** president, Morehouse College; author, *Breaking Through: The Making of Minority Executives in Corporate America*

"*Leadership Toolkit for Asians* is a masterful follow-up by the author who gave us pioneering insights about advancing Asian leadership in the workplace. This engaging book provides inspiration and a road map for Asians to bring their authentic selves to leading others. This is also a must-read for corporate leaders who want to build genuine multicultural leadership capabilities within their organizations."

—**STELLA NKOMO,** professor, University of Pretoria, South Africa; coauthor, *Our Separate Ways: Black and White Women and the Search for Professional Identity*

"Jane brings her commanding knowledge of culture and her intimate knowledge of the Asian American community to this essential read. Skillfully integrating relatable stories and self-assessments, she offers practical tools to translate ideas into action. I found this book transformative, providing essential insights for anyone seeking to grow their leadership skills in an authentic and meaningful way in a connected society."

—**HENRY ONG,** director of brand marketing, Universal Pictures

"Jane has had a profound impact in the DEI space. I have worked with her for many years and I am in awe of the knowledge, leadership, and compassion that she exudes. Jane brings her vast experience conducting qualitative research, cohort programs, and coaching thousands of Asian Americans and Asians in companies around the world. In a world where we have not reached parity for Asians in leadership, this book is an indispensable guide to breaking the bamboo ceiling once and for all."

—**MARY-FRANCES WINTERS,** founder and CEO, the Winters Group, Inc.; author, *Racial Justice at Work, Black Fatigue, We Can't Talk about That at Work,* and *Inclusive Conversations*

"*Leadership Toolkit for Asians* is a neat package of solid research, compelling exercises, and insightful guidance that will help Asian American leaders—and employers looking to act equitably and inclusively toward them—attain their potential."

> **—LILY ZHENG,** best-selling author, *DEI Deconstructed*; diversity, equity, and inclusion strategist

"Leading and influencing at work always involves balancing the tension between authenticity and adaptation, but this can be especially challenging for those of us different in culture or identity from our coworkers. With *Leadership Toolkit for Asians*, Jane Hyun enriches all of us with her wealth of knowledge and experience on the cultural complexities and nuances that shape inclusive leadership. The book presents potent strategies for Asian professionals and all who aspire to lead with authenticity to embrace and integrate one's cultural identities into one's leadership styles and to excel in the multicultural workplace. This is an essential read for anyone committed to fostering inclusive leadership for our globalized workforce."

> **—BERNARDO M. FERDMAN, PhD,** principal, Ferdman Consulting; editor, *Inclusive Leadership: Transforming Diverse Lives, Workplaces, and Societies*; distinguished professor emeritus, California School of Professional Psychology

"If you are an Asian American, or work with them, read this book. Jane Hyun has learned the hard way, and is here to smoothen your learning path. Her soul is in it, and she writes well. Jane has experienced cultural differences as a child, learned to understand them, and worked with them for over twenty years. I warmly recommend this book."

> **—GERT JAN HOFSTEDE,** professor, Wageningen University, the Netherlands; coauthor, *Cultures and Organizations* and *Exploring Culture*

"Jane has given us a precious gift. She's woven solid research and engaging stories into a fascinating account of the role of culture in leadership—a topic that we have not fully understood until now."

> **—OLEG KONOVALOV,** "the da Vinci of visionary leadership"; author, *The Vision Code*

"Leaders must carefully navigate their associates' differences and the complexities of their culture. Jane's stories of Asian American executives provide vivid examples on how to become culturally fluent and more effective, without compromising your integrity or authority."

> **—JAY STEINFELD,** founder and former CEO, Blinds.com; author of *Wall Street Journal* bestseller *Lead from the Core: The 4 Principles for Profit and Prosperity*

"*Leadership Toolkit for Asians* masterfully addresses the unique challenges faced by Asian Americans in the workplace, from shattering the 'model minority' myth to embracing cultural identity as a leadership strength. Its practical exercises and real-world examples offer a road map to personal and professional growth, making it an essential read for anyone looking to break through the bamboo ceiling with authenticity and resilience."

—**DAN FISHER, PhD,** managing partner, Contemporary Leadership Advisors; coauthor, *The End of Leadership As We Know It*

"With searing candor, Jane Hyun lays bare the challenges that Asian Americans face in the workplace in her new book, *Leadership Toolkit for Asians*. In the process Ms. Hyun presents real-life advice on how to overcome adversity and preconceptions. As such the Leadership Toolkit has applications to everyone in the workplace."

—**JOHN BALDONI,** member of 100 Coaches; author of many books on leadership, including his newest, *Grace under Pressure: Leading through Change and Crisis*

"As an adjunct professor of leadership at Columbia University and New York University, the incredibly important topic of diversity, equity, and inclusion is a central theme in my courses. And while we try to pay equal attention and respect to all demographic categories, the topic of leadership as it relates to Asians and Asian Americans is often overlooked. But thanks to Jane Hyun's wonderful new book, *Leadership Toolkit for Asians*, we now have a valuable new resource to help address this issue head-on. And, while written primarily for those of Asian descent, this book will also be of interest and value to allies, educators, and business leaders of all kinds as well."

—**TODD CHERCHES,** CEO, BigBlueGumball; author, *VisuaLeadership: Leveraging the Power of Visual Thinking in Leadership and in Life*

"Jane Hyun's *Leadership Toolkit for Asians*, a complement to *Breaking the Bamboo Ceiling: Career Strategies for Asians*, is a transformative guide that tackles the unique challenges faced by Asian professionals in Western work cultures. Hyun insightfully deconstructs the cultural barriers and provides actionable strategies to shatter them. Her authentic voice, combined with thought-provoking anecdotes, offers both inspiration and empowerment. This book is a leadership compass for every Asian professional seeking to decipher Western work culture and how to navigate it without losing authenticity—taking the best of both worlds. A very good use of time!"

—**ZEESHAN TARIQ,** senior vice president and chief information officer, Zimmer Biomet

"Leadership necessitates a deeper understanding of what it means to navigate differences and organizational biases in all their forms, including the 'bamboo ceiling.' Jane illuminates an important aspect of leadership that is often overlooked—this is required reading for anyone who wants to become a culturally fluent leader without compromising integrity or authority."

—**CHARLENE LI,** *New York Times* best-selling author, *The Disruption Mindset*

"Using sound, theory-based models and a practical hand, Jane helps us understand the complexities of culture and leadership. The stories of Asian American executives, who have each broken through barriers, make this book entirely readable and accessible, while teaching us important lessons."

—**JONAH BERGER,** marketing professor, Wharton School of the University of Pennsylvania; best-selling author, *The Catalyst*

"Everyone benefits when we all build a diverse network of relationships. And in this book Jane, an expert coach, shows you how the value of networks and community advances your career. She also shares strategies and tips for how to show up with impact on and off the screen."

—**CATHY PAPER,** president, speaker and coach, Networking4referrals.com

"As the owner of a marketing firm, author, and speaker, I read a lot of business books. I have to admit I forget many of them as soon as I've read them. Jane's book is different. Despite the specificity of the topic, *Leadership Toolkit for Asians* is full of leadership strategies that are applicable across the widest variety of situations. I can't wait to put them into practice."

—**MICHAEL F. SCHEIN,** founder, MicroFame Media

"Jane Hyun's groundbreaking work continues to pave the way for Asian American professionals. This book is a masterful blend of cultural insight and practical strategy, offering a unique and necessary perspective for anyone seeking to navigate and excel in today's complex corporate landscape. It's an essential resource for not only Asian Americans but also for anyone committed to diverse and inclusive leadership."

—**DORIE CLARK,** *Wall Street Journal* best-selling author, *The Long Game*; executive education faculty, Columbia Business School

"Navigating your way to leadership positions is challenging when you don't understand the terrain and you don't have the benefit of a guide. You are likely to encounter more obstacles as an Asian American due to systemic biases like the model minority myth.

Let Jane Hyun guide you by leveraging her personal experience and research to show you how to successfully navigate the terrain. I could see reflections of myself in the stories throughout the book, and anyone who aspires to reach the next level of leadership will benefit from the lessons found within."

—**JULIE KIM,** president, US Business Unit, Takeda Pharmaceuticals

"For the last twenty years, Jane has developed and applied data-informed insights to assist multicultural organizations through the application of cultural fluency in leadership. This new book provides critical tools to support Asian Americans as they advance in their leadership. Non-Asian leaders and colleagues of Asians will better understand the rich opportunities of having an inclusive organization and the advantages to becoming a culturally fluent leader. A must-read for HR leaders, chief diversity officers, [and] business leaders working in global organizations."

—**ELIZABETH NIETO,** chief diversity officer, Spotify

"*Leadership Toolkit for Asians* is a vital resource for Asian American professionals aiming to break through barriers and achieve their career goals. Jane's deep cultural insights and practical strategies provide a clear path to success in the workplace. This book empowers individuals to leverage their unique cultural strengths and equips organizations to foster diverse and inclusive environments. As someone deeply committed to leadership development, I wholeheartedly endorse this book as a valuable tool for personal and professional growth."

—**DR. MARSHALL GOLDSMITH,** Thinkers50 #1 executive coach; *New York Times* best-selling author, *The Earned Life, Triggers,* and *What Got You Here Won't Get You There*

"Beautifully written and packed with compelling stories from Asian professionals, *Leadership Toolkit for Asians* provides empowering advice and encouragement for leaders and aspiring leaders. Jane Hyun includes valuable tips, tools, and activities that Asian American workers, managers, and even executives can use to rediscover their unique perspective and lead authentically."

—**KEN BLANCHARD,** coauthor, *The New One Minute Manager*® and *Simple Truths of Leadership*

"The road to cultural fluency for any senior leader is largely uncharted and fraught with dynamic complexity. The wise leader searches out an 'expert guide' to help them navigate the many twists and turns on this road. Jane Hyun is the quintessential 'expert guide' across the full diversity spectrum. She has played and continues to play an indispensable role in my cultural fluency journey. In fact, I cannot imagine traveling this road without her. This latest work provides a new level of depth and breadth to her guidance. I wholeheartedly recommend it."

—**DOUGLAS R. CONANT,** *New York Times* and *Wall Street Journal* best-selling author; former CEO, Campbell Soup Company; former chair, Avon Products; founder, ConantLeadership

"Jane Hyun's *Leadership Toolkit for Asians* is your road map for skillfully navigating the workplace and leading a thriving professional life!"

—**LISA LING,** journalist, producer, and author

LEADERSHIP TOOLKIT FOR ASIANS

LEADERSHIP TOOLKIT FOR ASIANS

THE DEFINITIVE RESOURCE GUIDE FOR
BREAKING THE BAMBOO CEILING

JANE HYUN

Berrett–Koehler Publishers, Inc.

Berrett-Koehler Publishers, Inc.
1333 Broadway, Suite 1000
Oakland, CA 94612-1921
Tel: (510) 817-2277
Fax: (510) 817-2278
www.bkconnection.com

ORDERING INFORMATION
Quantity sales. Special discounts are available on quantity purchases by corporations, associations, and others. For details, contact the "Special Sales Department" at the Berrett-Koehler address above.
Individual sales. Berrett-Koehler publications are available through most bookstores. They can also be ordered directly from Berrett-Koehler: Tel: (800) 929-2929; Fax: (802) 864-7626; *www.bkconnection.com.*
Orders for college textbook / course adoption use. Please contact Berrett-Koehler: Tel: (800) 929-2929; Fax: (802) 864-7626.

Distributed to the U.S. trade and internationally by Penguin Random House Publisher Services.

Berrett-Koehler and the BK logo are registered trademarks of Berrett-Koehler Publishers, Inc.

Printed in the United States of America

Berrett-Koehler books are printed on long-lasting acid-free paper. When it is available, we choose paper that has been manufactured by environmentally responsible processes. These may include using trees grown in sustainable forests, incorporating recycled paper, minimizing chlorine in bleaching, or recycling the energy produced at the paper mill.

Library of Congress Cataloging-in-Publication Data
Names: Hyun, Jane, author.
Title: Leadership toolkit for Asians : the definitive resource guide for breaking the bamboo ceiling / Jane Hyun.
Description: First edition. | Oakland, CA : Berrett-Koehler Publishers, [2024] | Includes bibliographical references and index.
Identifiers: LCCN 2023053353 (print) | LCCN 2023053354 (ebook) | ISBN 9781523005758 (paperback) | ISBN 9781523005765 (pdf) | ISBN 9781523005772 (epub)
Subjects: LCSH: Minority executives—United States. | Career Development—United States. | Asian Americans—Employment. | Minorities—Vocational guidance—United States.
Classification: LCC HD38.25.U6 H98 2024 (print) | LCC HD38.25.U6 (ebook) | DDC 658.4/0973—dc23/eng/20231207
LC record available at https://lccn.loc.gov/2023053353
LC ebook record available at https://lccn.loc.gov/2023053354

First Edition
30 29 28 27 26 25 24   10 9 8 7 6 5 4 3 2 1

Book production: Happenstance Type-O-Rama
Cover design: Jiani Xiao, Agenda

엄마, 아빠

Min Hwan and Wha Ja Kim, my parents

*For showing what it means to be
fully known and yet fully loved.
And teaching me what lasts forever.*

*Abs and Tim, this one's for you,
though you might not realize it yet.*

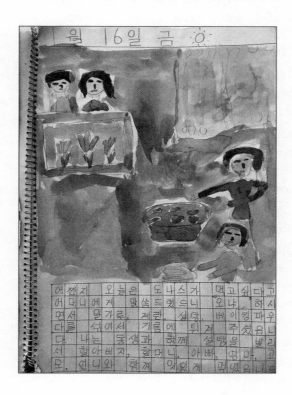

CONTENTS

PERSONAL NOTE FROM JANE

As a child in South Korea, the overwhelming mantra I heard was *Yeolsimhee*, which loosely translates to "You have to put your head down and work diligently in everything you do." In school, we were taught to show respect by quietly learning our lesson plans. If we tried to challenge the teacher, we were punished. When I moved to the United States and entered the New York City school system, I was shocked to see that my third-grade classmates were bold enough to contradict the teacher. Here, even at eight or nine years old, we were expected to speak up and share our own opinions on a topic. It was one of the first times I was encouraged to share my opinion freely.

Growing up Asian in America, you and I have experienced the daily conflict of having one foot in two very different worlds. We have grappled with how our cultural values are sometimes at odds with the dominant workplace culture. Even if you haven't experienced this challenge, you've wondered why others often have preconceived notions about your leadership capability. It has become the norm to try to figure out some mysterious path to get ahead in your company with few resources or a trusted guide to coach you. If this sounds like you, you're not alone.

In fact, Asian Americans are the least likely of any group to be promoted in corporate America. Asians make up 13 percent of the professional workforce, but only 3 percent of Fortune 500 corporate officers. The barriers holding us back are a complex set of social, cultural, and organizational issues without an easy solution. It's something I wrote about in my 2005 book, *Breaking the*

Bamboo Ceiling: Career Strategies for Asians, where I sought to challenge companies to proactively lead their talent with a multicultural lens while offering practical ways for Asians to advance in their careers.

Though I eventually learned to speak up and share my opinions as freely as my classmates did, there was still a voice inside my head screaming "Yeolsimhee!" in the face of authority figures. When I started working full-time, I recognized that there were unwritten rules that were clearly unknown to me, and I found that I didn't have access to the same resources that others did. There were a few minority development programs that provided access to insiders at prestigious organizations; however, most of these opportunities were not available to Asian American graduates entering the workplace.

Having dual messages drilled into my head from a young age was often confusing. And that confusion carried into my professional working life. Throughout different projects in those early years, I would receive occasional feedback about needing to be more vocal with my opinions, and I was often encouraged to speak up. Whether I was demonstrating it or not, I was keenly aware that Asian women were stereotyped as passive and quiet (these portrayals were reinforced daily in the media, if Asian women were depicted at all), and so I made a conscious effort in work settings to counteract that perception by voicing my opinions whenever I could.

A breakthrough moment came during an early performance review in my mid-twenties, when I was up for promotion to VP. An internal client who had neglected—despite my repeated requests—to provide essential data that I'd needed to complete my year-end report submitted a client review saying I was "too aggressive" in my approach. I was livid! I walked into his office and confronted him about it: "I have been living with the passive Asian female stereotype and everyone's biases toward me for years, and the feedback has been crystal clear: to speak up more, not less. I'm always operating under that narrative. Plus, your numbers were the only data point that was holding us up. Now you're telling me that I'm too aggressive?"

He backed off. He also apologized to my boss for his choice of words and said that the implication wasn't that I was doing a poor job, but that I was going after what I needed in a strong way. I got the promotion. However, that experience of having to defend my leadership capability made me realize how pervasive assumptions can be, and how much that was affecting both the way I acted in the workplace as well as other people's perceptions of me. I started to see patterns where I had been underestimated because of what I look like. I've also felt the frustration that comes from not having the right support or a clear path forward when it comes to advancing your career even after you've "proven yourself." Those feelings, along with those of the thousands of Asian professionals whom I've had the joy of coaching over the years, were the impetus that drove me to continue this work.

I've come to realize that we are not going to be most effective when we emulate the "white male executive" approach to leadership over the long term, and I have learned, through trial and error and lots of feedback from trusted advisors, to create my own path for working with and influencing others. I regularly speak with senior executives who tell me that they don't have the resources to fund leadership development programs for their Asian workers because it's not urgent. I've also had confidential one-on-ones with senior Asian leaders who are ambivalent about advocating for Asian Americans in their company because they don't feel connected to the greater Asian community and are not sure how they can serve as an executive sponsor.

This is why I've chosen to put together this resource guide: to give *you* that clear path forward when it comes to leading in your organization. I'll draw on my own experience of consulting with dozens of organizations that have adapted their internal processes and leadership expectations to create more equitable and inclusive workplaces. I'll also draw on my learning from hundreds of professionals whom I've interviewed or coached since *Breaking the Bamboo Ceiling* was published nineteen years ago. And I'll offer you practical advice while guiding you through a series of exercises that are designed to help you forge your own path as you lead.

The reality is that being Asian is far from a one-size-fits-all experience. Whether East Asian, South Asian, Southeast Asian, or Pacific Islander, we have all been socialized in our environments in complex and distinctive ways. Some of you, like me, grew up in Asia before moving to the United States. Perhaps you're a second- or third-generation Asian American, navigating what it means to bridge two cultures. Or, if you're starting out in your career, you might just be beginning to connect the dots with your identity and how others perceive your leadership effectiveness. It is important that we assess ourselves, delve deeper into our experience (even if some parts may be painful), and decide for ourselves how we want to work with others. By opening this book and choosing to do the work, you're one step closer to becoming the most authentic leader you can be.

HOW TO USE THIS TOOLKIT

Allow this book to be a living, breathing resource for you to write in, wrestle with, and reflect on. Work through it as if I were sitting with you, guiding you in your responses within each chapter.

Throughout this book, I will give you practical tools to carve out your own path and to identify ways to better access the skills and cultural knowledge you already possess. Instead of trying to "go along to get along" at your company, you'll learn to assert what you need from others and see the value of your unique bicultural perspective. You will learn how differences can be an asset to leverage for the good of your organization and the community. You'll bring a broader perspective to our society because of the multiple lenses through which you see the world.

It's not about putting your cultural values aside in order to excel in your workplace. Instead, it's about combining who you already are with new skills that will help you lead authentically in any professional environment.

I chose to write this book for our next generation, so that our kids can grow up in a world that sees them as bicultural people, where they can proudly say, "I am Asian *and* American," no matter their country of origin. I wrote it so that your skills can be appreciated and you can be understood for all that you are, not just as a stereotype. By doing this work, you will discover your value proposition. With that important tool, you can make your organization more innovative, sustainable, and profitable, which will be a win-win for all. In the end, you'll be in a better position to lead effectively by learning to embrace *all* of your complexities.

I encourage you to read through this book in multiple sittings. Read a few chapters, then put it down. After reflecting on its contents, talk about it with a friend, coach, or colleague. Work on an activity. Then pick it up again and read some more.

May this toolkit be the guide to unleash your potential. Let's do this!

NOTE If you are not yet familiar with the concepts of *Breaking the Bamboo Ceiling*, I encourage you to take a look. While it's not a prerequisite for this book, it will help you become fully informed on the cultural complexities of the Asian American experience.

Disclaimer

Except where affiliated with obviously identified corporations or organizations, names used in the book have been changed for anonymity.

"Asian employees/professionals" refers to Asian workers employed by the US labor force. Though most Asian professionals named in this book are Asian American, I've noted when an individual is based in another country.

Although *Asian American*, *APA* (Asian Pacific American), *AAPI* (Asian American and Pacific Islander), and *AANHPI* (Asian American, Native Hawaiian, and Pacific Islander) are all terms that have been used to describe the Asian American population in the United States, I've used *Asian American* throughout this book for simplicity's sake.

Professionals of color is a term used to describe Black or African American, Latino or Hispanic American, Asian American or Native Hawaiian and Pacific Islander, American Indian, or Alaskan Native employees in the workplace.

PART I

What It Means to Be a Leader in a Multicultural Society

1

THE BAMBOO CEILING AND YOU

What You Need to Know Now

Why This Book and Why Now?

"I don't worry about my Asian population here," said a diversity officer at a major global financial services firm a few years ago. "We're doing pretty well with them."

She looked so relaxed and sounded so self-assured as she spoke those words. She had approached me after I'd presented my findings at a Chief Diversity Officer leadership conference. I still remember feeling a nagging discomfort as we talked; I was disturbed that she felt she didn't need to address an entire population anymore. Based on my work over the last twenty years with dozens of Fortune 500 companies to close the gaps for their Asian workers, I begged to differ.

The truth is that Asian Americans face multiple barriers that keep them from leadership positions, but it's not a matter of not having the leadership skills in the first place. Instead, they might just *lead differently*. If a company doesn't know how to see that potential and nurture their development, then it's leaving unrealized value on the table.

Fast-forward to mid-March 2020. With a sinking feeling in my gut, I watched the news as America went into lockdown. I was sitting at the gate at the Minneapolis airport at the time, getting ready to board my flight, when I looked up and saw "China virus" flash across the CNN screen. Already, there were rumblings that Covid-19 was spreading. I knew that it was only a matter of time before the blame and anger toward Asians grew.

I was right. In the months that followed, there was a significant uptick in violence toward Asians. Between March 2020 and the end of 2022, more than 11,500 individual incidents of hate crimes against Asian Americans were documented. Events like the Atlanta spa shooting in 2021 and the Filipino woman stomped in Times Square made national headlines, but most events were underreported or overlooked, making even these large numbers look conservative. And who could forget the chancellor of Purdue University Northwest mocking an unintelligible Asian accent during commencement? That was a painful reminder that making fun of Asians is still socially acceptable.

After I wrote *Breaking the Bamboo Ceiling* in 2005, I hoped that professional spaces would become easier for Asian Americans to navigate. But sadly, that has not been the case. The rise of violence toward AAPI communities has been detrimental to their mental health and sense of safety. And the "model minority myth" (the misguided notion that Asians are all successful and have overcome the barriers to success) continues to persist. When Asians are targeted with such mockery, violence, and stereotyping, it makes it even more difficult for them to navigate a workplace that might butt up against the cultural ideals they were taught growing up.

Most people have no idea that Asians regularly face overt racial discrimination, let alone that they confront inequities throughout the corporate world. The model minority myth, by implying that Asians don't encounter discrimination and are all quite successful, often renders them invisible. This leads to fewer resources allocated for their community across organizations (including healthcare and government services), which can also make them feel like they're not being properly supported. Recent leadership studies have shown that Asian Americans don't feel like they belong in their workplaces, which further diminishes their mental health.

Since the 2020 murder of George Floyd and the subsequent growth of the Black Lives Matter movement, many companies have made a public vow of change, reworking their DEI (diversity, equity, and inclusion) policies and promising a more inclusive workplace. The increase in violence toward Asians in the past few years has been another wake-up call for organizations. But more often than not, their statements have been vague promises without clear, measurable solutions. The reality is that much work remains to be done to both improve organizational practices *and* equip Asian professionals with the tools to discover, define, and bring forth their distinctive leadership skills— skills that could be of great value to their employers.

While some of this work needs to be done at the higher levels, the change *can* start with you. But first you'll need to understand how you're currently showing up. Are you fully embracing your cultural differences and using them as a tool in how you lead? Or are you suppressing and assimilating in order to be accepted, without even realizing it?

In this chapter, we'll begin by looking at your current leadership approaches. From there, I'll provide exercises and questions to spur your creativity and out-of-the-box thinking, and guide you through a process that will help you imagine the leader you want to become. Finally, you'll brainstorm ways to enlist your organization (your manager, sponsor, or mentor) to partner with you in your development. You provide an openness to learning and a growth mindset, and I'll provide the tools and profiles of leaders who have tapped into deeper aspects of themselves to transform the way they work and lead.

You don't have to be a C-level leader who manages a hundred people to benefit from the tools you'll find here. The goal is to design and appreciate your own leadership models by delving deep into your cultural values, life experiences, and embedded approaches.

In chaotic, unpredictable times such as these, it can be hard to feel grounded. You can't predict when and if another pandemic will occur and rock your understanding of the world. But you can commit to personal growth and develop a keen understanding of yourself and how you want to grow and foster the tools within you, so that you're as prepared as possible for whatever life might throw your way.

By using this toolkit, you'll be able to develop the necessary skills to become a leader who integrates all parts of themselves. But doing so will require a deeper understanding of what it means to confront the bamboo ceiling—before learning how to shatter it for good.

Understanding the Bamboo Ceiling Today

Before you can determine the next step in your leadership journey and how you'll get there, you first need to know exactly where you are. This means having a grasp of your personal strengths, areas for improvement, and an overall snapshot of how you're perceived in your organization. But it also means, very importantly, where you stand given the current landscape—in business and in society as a whole. With that in mind, let's begin by reviewing the hard data that is out there for the Asian community: How are they viewed by others and what does the data reveal? How could it inform the way you advocate for your community, the mentors you seek, how you engage diversity efforts, and how you communicate your value proposition to your employers? While some of this data might be difficult or surprising to hear, it is important for you to understand. These truths inform your starting point.

Breaking the Bamboo Ceiling: Career Strategies for Asians brought the topic of Asian Americans in leadership to the diversity table and popularized the concept to a broader public audience for the first time. Back then, the Asian American population was an even smaller segment of the workforce. Since that book was released, an enormous amount of research has emerged that reinforces my initial findings. Asians are still excluded from leadership roles and are not being seen for their full contributions. This inability to make it fully through the system is a result of the organizational dynamics that keep them from being seen as leaders.

The bamboo ceiling is a combination of individual, cultural, and organizational factors that impede the career progress of Asians inside organizations. Yet it's not just about representation or counting the number of people in senior leadership. While it certainly includes barriers that keep them from the executive suites, it goes far beyond that to include structural biases that can keep them from being seen as leadership material.

The bamboo ceiling also reinforces the underlying assumption that "ideal" leadership template emulates the behaviors of men of European heritage. While there have been female CEOs and executives from various ethnic, racial, and cultural backgrounds who have made it into the boardrooms, by and large the leadership competencies that North American companies want you to emulate tend to discourage any variation in expressions of leadership. Women and people of color continue to be penalized when they don't "fit the mold" perfectly, while simultaneously being told that the workplace is a meritocracy so they just have to do their job well and things will fall into place.

One female executive in investment banking told me that her firm had hired a coach to help her with executive presence. She went into the meeting with an open mind. In the first session, she was asked, "Is there a philosophical reason why you don't wear makeup?" The conversation was less about how to get her contributions to be appreciated at the firm and more about her physical appearance.

It's important to note that while we delve into cultural challenges that affect the Asian community here, this is not a problem that can be solved solely by Asian workers. In order to make the workplace more inclusive and to bring out the best in *all* employees, anyone who works with Asians needs to grow in their cultural fluency as well.

The Three Phases of Leadership

In the course of conducting research for my first book, I interviewed one hundred executives from a variety of racial and cultural backgrounds (white, Black, Hispanic, Asian) to study their stories and to understand the journey they took from entry level to senior executive. It became clear that there are three distinct phases that leaders pass through as they move from entry level to senior level: producer, credibility builder, and organizational influencer (see figure 1-1). While unwritten rules can vary from industry to industry, my team and I found that these three phases were applicable to all the industries represented by those we spoke to.

The producer stage is the first phase of your career, and you may just be starting to manage people. What your company expects of you at this stage is to be reliable at working on your deliverables and producing what you are hired to do. By the second phase, credibility builder, it becomes increasingly important that you build strong relationships across the organization. By the third phase, the expectation is that as an executive of the organization, you are an influencer across the firm or organization, and that you think and act like an owner.

As you read on, start to reflect on how this breakdown applies to you and your career. What phase are you in right now? And what do you need to practice in order to move into the next phase of development? How might you demonstrate your value in terms of the other phases?

**Navigating the Unwritten Rules:
The Three Phases of Leadership**

Source: Hyun & Associates, executive insights interviews conducted by author

FIGURE 1-1. The three phases of leadership—entry level to senior level

What my team and I discovered was that it took Asian professionals the longest to move out of phase 1, often because they're so focused on "putting their heads down" and working hard—that is, being reliable producers. Not only that, the cultural values of discipline and diligence keep them from realizing the importance of demonstrating the attributes of the next phase of leadership: building credibility. After all, you've probably heard the adage that you can't wait until you get promoted to start acting like the boss.

In our work, once our clients realized that it was important to build relationships and credibility with different stakeholders, they learned to demonstrate those skills quickly. In egalitarian workplaces (such as in the United States), employees are encouraged to break out of their roles in order to maximize their potential and are rewarded for doing so (more about this in part II!). Unfortunately, many Asian executives didn't have the wherewithal early in their careers to make those adjustments until it came out as developmental feedback in a year-end performance review or after a colleague or manager called it out.

 Pause and Checkpoint

What phase of your leadership development do you find yourself in now? I call them "phases" because there is typically some overlap between the levels. Circle the phase you think most describes where you are now.

10/1/24

Phase 1   Phase 2   (Phase 3)

It's tough bc I'm an entrepreneur.

Who do you need in your corner to help you navigate the *next* phase?

Carolyn - assistant & social media mgr.
Mentors -

What skills do you want to learn?

Keynoting - improving bit by bit

Seven Key Findings—What Have We Learned?

Through our research of Asians in the corporate sphere, my team has discovered seven key issues that need to be addressed to fully realize the potential of Asian talent in organizations.

1) Asian Americans are far from being a *model minority* in corporate America, yet they're treated as one.

Biases continue to exist for Asians, but people outside the Asian community often don't recognize them, and even Asians can miss them. Therefore, stereotypes that are not being addressed, or are blatantly untrue, persist in the workplace and beyond. As noted earlier in the chapter, the model minority myth is the misguided perception that Asian Americans are a capable, hardworking, and docile group of people who have overcome barriers and no longer face discrimination. This has been used by the media and pundits to pit Asians against other racial groups.

A recent study from the National Science Foundation found that Asians encounter the highest rate of rejections, challenging the stereotype that they dominate academically. In the *New York Times*, Christina Yifeng Chen, a geoscientist at Lawrence Livermore National Laboratory, said, "There's this model minority myth that is a stereotype that suggests that Asians don't experience academic challenges." White scientists are generally more successful at winning federal research money from the National Science Foundation than Black, Latino, or other nonwhite scientists (see figure 1-2). Similarly, the success rate of proposals led by Asian scientists is about *20 percent below* the overall rate—a disparity that runs counter to the narrative that Asian Americans dominate the sciences and engineering fields.

Another study by Coqual found that while 25 percent of Asian professionals experienced bias and discrimination in the workplace, only 4 percent of white professionals thought they did.

In addition, many stereotypes toward Asian Americans are seen as positive, giving the false idea that Asians excel in academics or in the sciences and therefore do not face barriers to success. But the data proves otherwise.

These disparities have, unfortunately, continued to exist, reinforcing the idea that even if there are biases toward Asians, they're working in their favor. When Asians feel like their needs or pain points are invalidated, it is difficult for them to be fully seen in the workplace.

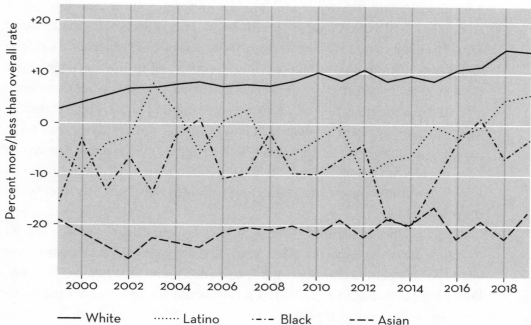

Racial Disparities in NSF Funding Rates

Source: C. Yifeng Chen, S. S. Kahanamoku, A. Tripati, R. A . Alegado, V. R. Morris, K. Andrade, and J. Hosbey, "Systemic Racial Disparities in Funding Rates at the National Science Foundation," *eLife* 11, no. e83071 (2022), https://doi.org/10.7554/eLife.83071.

FIGURE 1-2. Disparate success at the National Science Foundation

2) The Asian American population is not a monolith.

Asian Americans are often clumped together into one identity, when the demographics show that being Asian is an incredibly diverse and varied experience. The population comprises 23 million people, 20 countries, and even more dialects and subgroups. But because "Asian" is such a broad term, many Asian Americans feel that their individual experiences are not being recognized, particularly in the workplace, and are often confused for others.

For example, Priya, an Indian American woman in advertising, reported, "My VP often called me by the name of the Indian American woman who worked in creative. I actually work on the business side and we look nothing alike."

Huh?

The research shows this as well. A 2022 McKinsey study found that the 8.8 million Asian Americans are split across three main ethnic subgroups: East Asian, Southeast Asian, and South Asian. This wide-ranging distribution across industries and roles underscores the diversity of experiences among Asian American workers. They are overrepresented in low-paying occupations such as manicurist, skincare specialist, cook, and sewing machine operator. At the same time, they're also overrepresented in higher-wage technical fields, such as software development and computer programming. The large variance of wages between these occupation clusters means Asian Americans have the highest income inequality in the United States. An Asian American Federation study showed that one in four Asians in New York City lives below the poverty line.

There's a loss of identity when your boss or your client confuses you for the other Asian person in the office. You might ask yourself, *Do they even know what I do?* It's painful when you feel like you don't matter. When this dynamic is exacerbated without relief, it has a lasting impact on how engaged Asian employees are in the workplace.

📋 Checkpoint

How about you? Were you ever confused for another colleague of Asian descent in your workplace?

No but it happened at UC with Ahmed.

How did you respond?

I was shocked as we but nothing alte.

I was disappointed in how little profit we made

3) Asian professionals operate in a very narrow band of "acceptable behaviors" in the workplace.

Many Asians feel the need to edit themselves or hide their cultural differences (including minimizing their accents and other attributes) to be perceived as effective in the workplace. A recent study, Asians in America, found that Asians were the least comfortable "being [them]selves" in the corporate workplace.

In my firsthand experience running leadership coaching programs for Asian Americans, I found that nearly half of the participants I worked with were born in Asia and still carry deeply embedded cultural values from their country of origin. Multinational companies prefer a leadership style that reflects the needs of the corporate headquarters, which are typically located in North America. If you are an applicant who might not be perceived as "aggressive" or capable of promoting your accomplishments, you will be seen as ineffective. One Chinese American lawyer was told that he needs to operate with more of an "effortless swagger" like the partners. Fitting into the corporate system can come at the cost of suppressing who you are.

Asian women experience a double dilemma: those who are extroverted or outspoken report getting feedback from managers and colleagues that they are "too aggressive," while those who are more reserved in demeanor get penalized for "not speaking up."

It's damned if you do, damned if you don't.

4) As a result of the increase in violence toward Asian Americans, they are experiencing increased levels of stress and mental health issues.

The 2023 Strangers at Home study, which documented the daily indignities of racism and microaggressions for Asian Americans, shows evidence of a broken career pipeline. Nearly two out of three Asian professionals said that the ongoing violence against the AAPI community has negatively impacted their mental health, and 62 percent said that it has decreased their feelings of safety while commuting to work. Additionally, 50 percent said it has diminished their ability to focus at work, and one in three Asian and Asian American professionals said they have experienced racial prejudice at their current or former companies.

My own friends have told me that they are afraid to commute on public transportation throughout the country. I have felt this fear as well. In a chaotic and uncertain time, it's another thing to worry about when you don't know when and if you can leave the house to run an errand, let alone report to the office. Without having this acknowledged or improved, Asians are facing a constant daily battle that is unlikely to resolve itself.

5) Asian employees are not adequately recognized by organizational diversity initiatives and are therefore underresourced.

In my own research, I found that affinity group networks that focus on Asian American employees' needs are underresourced. Corporate leaders often have good intentions of supporting our community and might even express their commitment verbally, but they offer little funding and advocacy to make that intention a reality. I've even had large companies ask if I could work or speak for free. Time and time again, I've seen how little funding Asian resource groups get.

The Strangers at Home study backs this up. It found that while Asians are getting hired and recruiters are happy to bring them in, they're entering a system that's indifferent or hostile to the way that they show up, or they're not provided with the necessary support to advance through the career lifecycle. Asian employees end up spending a great deal of effort trying to fit into the system and not bringing their authentic selves to the workplace.

6) Asians lack sponsors who could advocate for them and provide access to future opportunities.

An important discovery I've made while conducting leadership interventions in companies is that you can't advance Asian talent by just "fixing the Asians." A supportive management structure, combined with sponsors and mentors, is an *absolute* requirement.

However, the Strangers at Home study found that Asian and Asian American professionals are the least likely of any racial group surveyed (29 percent) to say they have role models at their company, the least likely to say they have strong networks (17 percent), and the least likely to have a sponsor (21 percent). Due to underrepresentation in senior roles, lack of role models, and thin support networks, Asians have few if any advocates in powerful positions to help their career advancement.

Many Asians lack access to exclusive networks, which keeps them from high-profile projects and "insider track" knowledge. This is also backed up by my own research. For fifteen years at Hyun & Associates, my team and I have asked Asian professionals in our leadership coaching programs if they had sponsors in their organization. We defined sponsors as senior leaders (not necessarily their direct managers) who were advocates for their careers. We distinguished the role of sponsor from mentors (who provide career advice, general support, and guidance about organizational politics). Only 15 percent of the mid-career professionals we polled had sponsors. Sponsors are influential executives who are willing to "put in one of their chips" in your favor in spaces and places where you don't have entry. In most organizations, it is very difficult to get ahead without a sponsor. The majority of people we worked with had mentors, but not sponsors.

This created a gap in the workforce and made it increasingly difficult for Asians to rise into leadership roles. Without an influential sponsor, you will never get the access you need to gain entry to the next level of leadership.

Your Turn

Do you have a mentor?   Yes   (No)

Do you have a sponsor?   Yes   No

If not, how has it kept you from navigating your career? *If i seo*

a big hondrance .

And if so, how has it helped you in attaining your career objectives?

7) Asians often feel like they don't belong in the workplace.

The Power of Belonging study conducted by Coqual in 2020 found that Asian women, Black women, and Asian men had the lowest levels of "belonging" in their workplace. Asian women had the lowest levels of belonging when compared with all ethnic/racial groups. To better identify the building blocks of belonging, the study grouped twenty-four items that characterized belonging into these four categories:

- **Seen:** Does the organization recognize and value my contributions?

- **Connected:** Do I have positive, authentic interactions with others?

- **Supported:** Does the organization provide the support to get my work done?

- **Proud:** Do I feel aligned to the purpose of the organization, and not just like a "cog in the wheel"?

Feeling like you don't belong can have a severe impact on your day-to-day functioning on the job and on your mental health.

This finding was supported by a 2022 Bain study called the Fabric of Belonging. The survey showed there is a critical need for greater workplace inclusivity for Asian American workers. Asian men and women feel the least included of all the demographic groups Bain surveyed. However, less than 30 percent of employees across all geographies, industries, and demographic groups say they feel fully included at work. Asian workers report feeling the least included, with only 16 percent of Asian men and 20 percent of Asian women saying they felt fully included at work.

This lack of acceptance can create a gap where Asian workers, by trying to "fit into the norms," are wasting valuable time and energy that would be better spent on creating innovative solutions.

Accelerating the development of Asians in organizations requires these seven issues to be addressed. And it will require more than just Asians trying to develop new skills and going out of their comfort zones to work effectively. Instead of conforming to the existing models, we need to rethink and redesign what leadership competence looks like for a multicultural, global workforce.

Asian American leaders bring strong language and cultural acumen that can be a hidden competitive advantage for companies looking to thrive in a diverse marketplace. Asians need a new way to express their leadership, and their colleagues and managers need a new way to see their Asian populations. We need a wide-angle lens to accommodate a variety of leadership approaches. And that's exactly what I'll be walking you through in this book.

Bottom Line

What resonates with you after you learned about the latest research on Asians and leadership development? *White ppl confy*

PoC who lead different

_____

What specific experiences have you had that align with or counter the key findings above?

_____

_____

How might you personally pivot as a leader in light of this data? What would you do differently at your organization?

_____

_____

2

WHERE ARE YOU ON THIS JOURNEY?

Progress Made; Still a Long Way to Go

Whenever I sit down with a new client, we embark on a series of self-reflective activities to take stock of their leadership health. In that process, I also obtain insights from their close work colleagues, since I'm not always there to see them in action. I do this to help my clients begin examining how they're showing up in their professional lives, and to gain an accurate reading of their modus operandi before we begin to work on their larger aspirational goals.

One huge aha moment that I've witnessed repeatedly with my clients is when they become fully aware of how culture impacts their workplace behavior. For example, while I was group coaching a few leaders in a consumer products company, one Chinese American leader consistently used "we" and not "I" to describe her most significant win upon completing a project. It wasn't until I pointed it out that she realized she'd been avoiding using "I," even though she was the lead person driving the project to completion.

Raised in a Confucian-influenced home along with its gender norms, this leader had not been encouraged to promote herself in the presence of authority figures or more experienced colleagues, and this, coupled with her sense of modesty and tendency to acknowledge the group effort rather than her own accomplishments, was surfacing at work in subtle ways. *It wasn't just my project—we did it as a group!* When presenting her findings to a senior leader (who was used to hearing people take credit for everything), she realized that her choice of words wasn't the most effective at highlighting her hard-earned contributions.

It can be difficult to recognize the way that cultural nuances shape who we are; after all, we don't typically recognize culture until we're put in an environment that's at odds with our assumptions. And if we haven't yet been confronted with evidence that our leadership or workplace style is not working, then why would we do anything about it? It makes sense, then, that you might not have put much thought into your cultural influencers—and that's okay. When you're operating in a dominant culture that limits how you can show up, it's difficult to imagine another way of leading.

Becoming authentic in your leadership has to start with an awareness of your core values. How have your unique background and socialization influenced how you show up in the workplace? And how aware are you of those differences?

In this chapter, we'll begin the process of identifying your unique cultural influences while asking the question: What does being Asian mean to you? To start to unpack that, we'll need to break down the larger systemic realities of what Asian American professionals encounter in the workplace, and how those might be subtly affecting how you show up every day. As you hear other leaders' stories and reflect on your own experiences, begin naming where and how these factors affect your own life. The activities sprinkled throughout the chapter will help you start that necessary self-inventory. By the end of the chapter, you'll understand that although progress has been made, there's still a long way to go—and you can be part of accelerating that change.

What Does It Mean to Be Asian American?

Alena Brown, the director of Sourcing & Procurement, Digital Transformation at PepsiCo, remembers the sting of growing up in Pittsburgh and looking different from others around her. Her mom was Chinese, and Alena stood out in her not-very-diverse neighborhood. Most kids assumed at first that she was either Latina or Hawaiian, not half Chinese. They struggled to "categorize" her . . . as if a person's complex sense of self can be put in a box!

People often assume things about Asian Americans based on outside appearance without taking the time to really understand who they are. This can become more complicated if you, like Alena, are straddling two different cultures. "My mom was always about not creating too many waves . . . not being the 'loudest duck that gets shot,' unless there was something that absolutely needed to be said," but, Alena recalls, "my dad always said I should try to stand out." This complex sense of identity can be incredibly complicated to navigate, particularly when those around you aren't doing the work to better understand the nuances of your experience.

What makes a person Chinese American (or Asian American) anyway? Is it about outward appearance, or it is a journey to a healthy ownership of who you want to be, on your own terms? Or both? The truth is that identity is not just about what you look like on the outside; it's about how you see yourself, your deeply held cultural values, and how you choose to *embody* those values in everyday life. Only you can define your Asian American identity to the world.

For Alena, discovering her identity meant drowning out the noise of her peers and focusing on the cultural values that mattered to her. She had to come to a healthy ownership of who she wanted to be, in her own time and on her own terms. Alena recalls: "I come from a long line of strong women on my mom's side, and my dad also encouraged me to take on challenges. When I was bullied as a kid, while it was tough, it helped me find myself and helped me position myself to stand my ground in who I was and who I wanted to be." Her parents instilled in her the importance of learning Mandarin at an early age. "As an adult, now I appreciate being different. Today, when I'm in a room with other Chinese colleagues and call people out by recognizing when they speak Chinese, they're like, *Whoa! How do you know our language*?!"

> *Identity is not just about what you look like on the outside, it's about how you see yourself, your deeply held cultural values, and how you choose to embody those values in everyday life.*

While Alena's bicultural identity wasn't easy to maneuver in her youth, it's now a workplace strength. The work she's had to do to navigate audiences with very different points of view has helped exercise her empathy and emotional intelligence muscle. There is power in both perspectives: the intersection of the hardships she dealt with in her youth and the unique cultural perspective she brings to her leadership at PepsiCo. "When you walk into a room, you know—right off the bat—the perception of you. I can pick up on nonverbals; I know how to read a room. That's my cultural value proposition. I'm not [on] one side or another, I'm actually in the middle so I can understand and see what other people don't see as important and I [can] call it out if I need to."

Through her experiences, Alena has learned how to build and shape authentic relationships—and that's *powerful*.

—

There are many variations to being Asian American, and there's no right or wrong way to engage within your organizational culture, but Asian Americans are often made to think there is and rewarded for adapting to the dominant culture's expectations. If that continues, it often starts to mute their unique perspectives and can keep them from using their unique cultural strengths as assets. And that means that others lose out because they don't experience the fullness of what Asian American workers can do.

Is Your Organization Viewing You through a Multicultural Lens?

The past few years have brought increased awareness of the biases that Asian Americans experience. But the cold reality is that most organizational leaders do not yet possess enough cultural fluency to see the potential leadership qualities that Asian Americans can bring—particularly because Asian Americans might lead *differently*.

Most organizational leaders do not yet possess enough cultural fluency to see the potential leadership qualities that Asian Americans can bring—particularly because Asian Americans might lead differently.

Look at Alena, who learned to deal with insensitive comments that tried to put her in a box. Her experience with bullying actually helped her build resilience and later gave her an extra dose of empathy to work effectively with her team members.

She's not a pushover either—she knows how to have tough conversations when necessary. This is not to say that it will be easy for you to grapple with the complex, multicultural identity of what it means to be Asian American—especially since there are so many ways that being Asian in America can show up. But in order for you to use your own unique cultural experience to your advantage, it's important to recognize the ways *your* background has shaped you, and to start to consider how it can help inform your leadership capabilities in positive ways.

In part II, we'll dive deeper into how different dimensions of culture have affected your personal approach to leadership. But for now, I want you to begin the process of unpacking your past experiences.

 ## Dig Deeper: Alena's Story

1. Review Alena's leadership story and put a star next to the top three passages that resonate with you.

2. Do any of her specific experiences remind you of your own or those of your friends, whether at your organization or in your personal life? Jot the name of the person in the margin or simply write "Me."

3. Underline three powerful words that leap out at you in her story.

4. If you could ask Alena one question, what would it be?

The Many Faces of the Asian Community

As you've probably gathered from both Alena's story and your own experiences, even the question "What does it mean to be Asian/Asian American?" needs to be interrogated a bit. After all, it seems to assume that there's a single response to the question instead of a multiplicity depending on your perspective.

Growing up Asian in America, I lived through my own version of this internal duality.

The Korean culture I grew up in could be very group-oriented. In that setting, you never acted alone. Whatever you did or said was a reflection on your parents, your extended family, and even your larger community. I used to resent that while growing up in the US and I often wished that I could just date whoever I liked or act however I wanted. As a teenager, I felt burdened by these constraints, even as I tried to navigate this duality with my family and community. I watched my non-Asian friends putting their personal interests above others, free to do whatever they wanted to do on the weekend instead of going to Korean school or visiting family.

But that experience, while fraught with conflict, also taught me something.

Working in corporate America, I discovered that a collective mindset could be beneficial when building, strengthening, and performing as a team, especially when coupled with a sense of urgency. And when I started coaching Asian leaders, I realized that I wasn't alone. Many of the Asian leaders I worked with would seek outside perspectives early in their decision-making that would help them later in the implementation phase of projects. Once we could see our own cultural values from a nonjudgmental point of view, these values made a lot of sense and were actually really helpful to our effectiveness!

My experience is not necessarily unique among Asian Americans, but it's not universal either. It's not a simple task to define "Asian American" because the term itself is not one race, ethnic group, or cultural community. The Pew Research Center (2023) reports that of the Asian adults who live in the US, 51.53 percent say that they most often describe themselves using identifiers that reflect their heritage and family roots, either alone or together with "American" (see figure 2-1). Given that more than 68 percent of adult Asians in the US are immigrants and probably a good number are children of immigrants, the cultural values instilled in them by their parents remain fresh in their memory and part of their psyche. Many grew up with parents who didn't

How Asian Adults in the US Identify

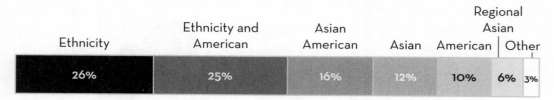

52% use ethnicity alone, or in combination with American.
51% use American alone, or in combination with ethnicity or Asian.

Asian American	Asian
16%	12%

28% use Asian alone, or in combination with American.

While half of Asian adults in the US identify most often by their ethnicity, many other labels are also used to express Asian identity in the US.

Source: Hyun & Associates with data from N. G. Ruiz, L. Noe-Bustamante, and S. Shah, "Diverse Cultures and Shared Experiences Shape Asian American Identities," May 8, 2023, Pew Research Center.

FIGURE 2-1. Identity preferences of Asian adults (percentages rounded for simplicity)

speak English perfectly or who weren't always able to engage with their American teachers in the way they wanted them to.

In general, Asians are a diverse population. While there are dozens of languages and dialects spoken, a large range of religious diversity, and over twenty distinct nationalities in the United States, 79 percent of the Asian American population (as of the 2020 Census) are represented by six nationalities: Vietnamese, Korean, Indian, Chinese, Japanese, and Filipino (see figure 2-2). They are loosely categorized as South Asian (Indian, Pakistani, Bangladeshi, etc.), Southeast Asian (Vietnamese, Cambodian, Thai, Filipino), East Asian (Chinese, Japanese, Korean), and Pacific Islander.

Asian Ethnicities in the United States

Other Asian Ethnicities

Pakistani	2%
Thai	2%
Cambodian	2%
Hmong	1%
Laotian	1%
Taiwanese	1%
Bangladeshi	1%
Nepalese	1%
Burmese	1%
Indonesian	1%
Sri Lankan	<1%
Malaysian	<1%
Mongolian	<1%
Bhutanese	<1%
Okinawan	<1%

Chinese 24
Indian 21
Filipino 19
Vietnamese 10
Korean 9
Japanese 7
Other Asian Ethnicities 15

Source: Hyun & Associates with data from N. G. Ruiz, L. Noe-Bustamante, and S. Shah, "Diverse Cultures and Shared Experiences Shape Asian American Identities," May 8, 2023, Pew Research Center.

FIGURE 2-2. Asians are not a monolith

Part of the struggle of being Asian in America is that Asians often get clumped into one big category—as if all of their experiences are the same.

When Kim Cummings, an HR executive at a children's hospital, meets people for the first time, she usually gets asked, "What are you?" They will then guess a mixture of every Asian American background or country of origin imaginable. But for Kim, as well as many others, identity is not one-sided. "While I was born and raised in Korea, I identify as Korean Mexican American. . . . Coming to the States has inspired me to explore my Hispanic identity." Kim's cultural story is complex and not one that is easily categorized, and this means she has had to grapple with integrating the different cultural parts of her rich heritage.

For Ben Hires, the CEO of Boston Chinatown Neighborhood Center, identity has also been a complex journey. Though he now serves the Boston Asian community, Ben grew up in a white family in rural New Jersey after being adopted from South Korea. "I do say I am Asian, but culturally I don't have a strong sense of being Asian the way my (Taiwanese) wife does." Both Kim and Ben have experienced the complexity around identity—and the disconnect that can happen when others see you differently from how you see yourself. But does that make either of them any less Asian? No.

The truth is that your story encompasses many different variables. More salient than your country of origin, year of immigration, or the language you speak is how much of your cultural identity is tied to your heritage and how you embody that in your day-to-day life.

You can identify as Asian in a myriad of ways no matter how you choose to define what it means to be Asian.

 ## Your Turn: Identifying Your Identity

- How do you identify? (Who's your "tribe"?) Feel free to cite how you refer to yourself with or without your country of origin.

  _____

  _____

- Do you see yourself as Asian American or [country of origin] American (e.g., Indian American, Vietnamese American, Japanese American)? Does it make a difference for you in the workplace? Why or why not?

  _____

  _____

Where Are You From? The Perpetual Foreigner Syndrome

In exploring what it means to be Asian American, it doesn't help that so many in the community have been subjected to messaging that distorts, dismisses, or "others" their identity.

When I was in college, I remember being told, "Wow, you speak English so well!" At the time, I felt proud hearing that, because at one point in my life, I literally hadn't been able to speak the language. Later, I realized that assuming I wouldn't be able to speak English because of the way that I look is a microaggression often directed at Asians. It's something that has followed me throughout my life: the idea that no matter how integrated I am in American culture, I will always be an outsider. A few years ago, after I spoke at a small conference in Washington, DC, someone came up to me and said, "You speak perfect English! Like wow." I don't think she made that comment to any of the other speakers. I responded with, "I'm glad you think so—I've been working on it for forty years!"

The *perpetual foreigner* syndrome is the ongoing perception that Asian Americans are aliens, regardless of how long they've been living in the United States.

Look at what happened to Japanese Americans during World War II. Despite being citizens in this country for years, whole families were forcibly moved into internment camps, where many lost everything they had worked for. Did the same thing happen to German Americans? No, because their outward appearances didn't automatically mark them as "different" from white Americans. Asians' "otherness" as Americans often makes them a target when the country is engaged in conflicts and reinforces the idea that they will forever be outsiders.

The Asian American Workplace Experience since Covid-19

The stereotype of the forever foreigner was reinforced when people were looking for someone to blame for the Covid-19 virus. Suddenly, certain news outlets were calling it the "China virus," and the country saw an escalation in crimes against Asian Americans as anger and fear grew. Asian Americans were instantly viewed as foreigners rather than as fellow citizens also trying to survive the deadly pandemic. Jeremy Lin, a basketball player and advocate for the Asian community, recounted being asked by security guards on his way to the team bus, "Where do you think you're going? Where's your pass?" Given the paucity of Asian Americans in pro basketball, they couldn't believe that he was there to play for the Raptors. He would also get called "coronavirus" on the court.

You might speak perfect English without an accent, but it often doesn't matter: Asians are still attacked or discriminated against for what they look like in a country where they've been for all or most of their lives. And because of this "foreigner status," they have an extra challenge when it comes to being seen as leaders. To some extent, Asians need to prove that they are fit to lead in a way that their white counterparts do not.

The Model Minority Myth and How It Shows Up Today

As if being perceived as the perpetual foreigner doesn't make life difficult enough, Asian Americans have another harmful stereotype to deal with.

In the previous chapter, we dug into how the model minority myth (MMM) refers to the misguided perception that Asians are a hardworking, capable, docile group who have overcome all barriers and no longer face discrimination. Yet we know this isn't true.

I remember first hearing that *Crazy Rich Asians* was coming out as a feature film. While I was happy to support a Hollywood movie with an all-Asian cast (the first since *Joy Luck Club* in 1993!), in the back of my mind, I was worried that it would perpetuate the stereotype that all Asians are wealthy and don't have any needs. This highlights the underlying question behind the MMM: *What are you complaining about anyway? If about 50 percent of Asians graduate from college, what's the big deal?*

The big deal is that we know the MMM isn't true, but it still provides an easy out for organizations to ignore their Asian populations. This results in Asian groups (e.g., ERGs) being underfunded, and their real issues being neglected.

These subtle exclusions by leadership and the assumption that Asians don't have any needs in the workplace can happen because Asian workers do not always voice the incidents of discrimination or career snubs they experience. While some of this silence might be cultural, it's also important to recognize that it's not your fault—you are working under a system that is much larger than just one individual. Still, in the long term, this lack of awareness by organizations leads to eroded employee engagement, emotional damage, and professional harm. Asians have felt this stinging wound for years but might have lacked the voice to communicate it. One of the goals of this book is to help you start to identify where the MMM has affected you personally and how you can work to combat it in your own workplace. The following activity represents an important first step in that direction.

Identifying and Assessing the Impact of the Model Minority Myth (MMM)

1. Do you think your CEO and the executive leadership team can name the value of the Asian employee population and its relevance for your organization's priorities and business?

    ___ Yes ___ No

    If yes, how do they show that they value this population?

    _____

If no, what could increase their awareness of this critical demographic?

_____

2. How does the MMM surface in your industry? (If it doesn't, explain why you think this is so.)

_____

3. How does your organization stack up against others in your industry when it comes to diversity and inclusion efforts?

_____

4. As a follow-up to #3, how does your organization's support of Asian employees reflect or diverge from the industry's as a whole?

_____

5. Are Asian employees considered in conversations about diverse talent advancement and succession planning conversations?

___ Yes ___ No

If no, what role do you think the MMM plays in this absence?

_____

6. Does your organization focus on Asian professionals in its hiring and selection efforts at all levels? Are Asian professionals considered "overrepresented" at any level?

_____

7. Do you have an Asian network or employee resource group (ERG) in your organization?

___ Yes ___ No

8. Does the Asian network/ERG receive adequate funding for its events and strategic initiatives?

___ Yes ___ No

If yes, is there any support that it does not receive?

_____

If no, how could the MMM be one of the causes?

_____

9. How involved are the Asian employees in the Asian ERG? Describe their attitude toward it (feel free to cite your own experience or comments you've heard from others).

_____

The Meaning of Our Names

Names in Asian families are critical. They represent the hopes and dreams of the parents, and the family legacy is carried on in the names they give their children. In Korean families, the first or second part of your name could be the same as that of your siblings. In my family, the name almost always refers to birth order. My dad's name is Min Hwan and his younger brothers are In Hwan, Hong Hwan, and Il Hwan. Leaving out one of the syllables changes the meaning of the name. Too often, people in the US see the first name, which is written after the surname, as the middle name. As other examples, the Indian name Aditi (the mother of the gods) means "boundless or limitless" in Hindi, and Ahad means "one, unique, match-less." Mispronouncing or misspelling either name loses a part of its core essence. Too many Asians have experienced the "otherness" that comes with having their names mispronounced.

When I get invited to events to speak about cultural fluency, there's usually an executive who moderates the Q&A that follows the session. From experience, I've learned to tell people how to pronounce my name ahead of time. If I don't volunteer it, I find that people are hesitant to ask or they don't even think to until they're stumbling over my name in front of five hundred people. Telling them up front doesn't always solve the problem, but it is a practice that helps and one I've incorporated into our logistics calls for my events.

Names are connected to cultural histories. Names *matter*. And having someone mispronounce them or not bother to learn them is another way that Asians are an afterthought for mainstream culture. By understand-ing what your name means and what your parents wanted you to inherit through it, you can start to explore who you are and to delve into the meanings and sources of strength that come from your heritage. You can start to answer: *Who do you want to be, and how are you going to make that happen?*

📋 Checkpoint

Have people (teachers, bosses, coworkers, clients) ever mispronounced your first name or last name?

_____

If they did, how did you respond?

_____

How might you respond in the future if this occurs?

_____

Indeed, navigating these complexities—not being seen as your true self, having your name mispronounced, being misunderstood—can be exhausting. In the midst of that journey, it's important to think about how your cultural experiences could be *an asset to your leadership*, something that can help you become a strong leader in your own right. In order to get to that point, however, you'll need to do the work of digging in deep, being vulnerable about your lived reality, and examining who you are and how you can show up as your most authentic self.

Navigating the Work of Personal Growth and Transformation

What is this bringing up for you? How are you taking this all in?

You've gotten in touch with your identity and what that means in today's workplace, so let's shift gears a bit and focus on how to create a compelling future. After all, that's the purpose of this book—not just to identify the cultural factors that can impede or boost your career development but also to help you be an active force in your own leadership conversation.

Removing Barriers and Achieving Personal Breakthroughs

Sustained change doesn't happen when it's forced on you. People change only when they want to, in the areas where they want to change. And this responsibility isn't just on the individual: organizations **and** your leaders have their part to do too, since your career success does not exist in a vacuum. In her book *The Last Word on Power*, Tracy Goss delves into the process of reinvention that a company's leaders must undergo before any organizational transformation can happen.

As I write this, I am very conscious of the underlying burden on women and people of color in the United States, who often have to work harder to "make it," as well as the pervasive idea that if they don't, it's their fault despite the barriers in their path. It's easy to think that Asians are the ones who need to change and the only ones who own their development. But this is not about fixing you; this is about continued growth. There's nothing wrong with you, and it's not solely your responsibility to create change.

A huge part of what I've learned in helping organizations navigate diversity is that no matter how much people of color strive, no matter how much they show up and ask for a seat at the table, they're not going to make it if those in power don't give them access to that table. This access includes mentoring and advancement opportunities.

So when I refer to the journey of personal change, I'm not discounting the work that needs to happen on a systemic level. But for Asians, the journey of personal change means discovering that part of yourself that can be shifted to create transformative results for you in your organization, career, personal life, home life, and more. Any venture worth embarking on requires such a shift— and by extension, a shift in others' response to you. Getting to your ultimate vision is about digging deep, with empathy and emotional resilience, to do the work that is set for you as a person from a nondominant culture.

In order to create your ideal self, I want you to go in with eyes wide open about the work this will entail and to be real about the obstacles you might encounter. In order to achieve great things, you need to have the organization behind you. I firmly believe that *you* can be the change agent for innovative ideas and outcomes in your organization!

As the other important part of this equation, the organization, your colleagues, and your managers will need to adjust and practice adaptive leadership with you to meet you where you are. Let's examine how they're currently seeing you and how you're showing up for others in your daily life. How do you get an accurate view of how others see you?

Learning How You're Perceived by Others

As you develop your own leadership model, you may find it helpful to complete a multifactor feedback assessment (360-degree feedback) to identify how others perceive you. As I mentioned at the start of the chapter, in a full coaching program, I seek valuable perspectives from my clients' close work colleagues and stakeholders. While perceptions are not always reality, in organizational settings, the way you're viewed by other people—especially those who are critical to your development—may give you an idea of how you show up in the world.

Whenever I coach MBA students in their late twenties, they'll often say to me, "I took this 360 in the first two or three weeks of classes. They don't really know the real me!" Perhaps this is true, but I like to remind them that while the way you're viewed by your peers may evolve throughout the semester, the first impression you send out to your fellow students at the start of the term tells them something about your persona, and it's a quick read you should pay attention to. If you don't have access to a coach, you can also ask a few trusted advisors who know your work well to provide feedback about you. However you obtain the feedback, the goal is to gain an objective-as-possible snapshot of your strengths and areas for improvement.

While engaging with this book, I want you to articulate your own personal vision for your leadership. Then, you'll create a personalized leadership model that will describe how you want to impact the world around you. Throughout that process, you will also identify people who will keep you accountable to those goals and help you bring that model to life.

I have found that when you have a meaningful, exciting vision to pursue that you care deeply about, you'll be motivated to do whatever it takes to get there.

Recognizing Your Inner Voices

To lead courageously, you must confront the voices in your head that discourage you or prevent you from moving forward. These fears are usually unspoken, but many people—including some of the most influential leaders—deal with them when trying to accomplish something big.

Whenever you're about to embark on a meaningful activity or new venture (see your vision from chapter 1), it is bound to be coupled with risk. Think about it: when you were last embarking on a new exercise routine, how easy was it to revert to turning on Netflix instead of going out for that walk? Without maintaining good habits, guardrails, and a supportive community of people to hold you accountable, you won't be able to practice the leadership behaviors you want to demonstrate. The work of influencing and motivating others takes a great deal of mental and emotional energy—you have to learn to manage yourself and surround yourself with the support you need.

What inner voices are competing inside your head?

 ## Identifying Your Inner Voices: A Checklist for Self-Reflection

When you're feeling unmotivated or stuck, what is the general message your internal monologue is sending you? Check all that apply.

☐ Fear of failure

☐ Fear of imperfection

☐ Fear of success

☐ Fear of losing face

☐ Fear of losing security

☐ Hesitation/inaction

Key Learning Points

Before we move on, let's review the key items just discussed.

- As you develop your leadership approach, consider specific workplace experiences that have impacted you or shaped your behavior.

- The Asian American community is not a monolith. You have your own unique perspective and heritage, and only you can define your own identity.

- Consider how the perpetual foreigner syndrome and the model minority myth show up in your organization. How are Asian employees viewed?

- Listen to your inner voices—the authentic ones—and be mindful of the fears and uncertainties that can get in your way.

PART II

Bringing Your Full Self to Work

3

YOUR VISION

What Do You Want Your Leadership Approach to Be?

The most personal is the most creative.

—**BONG JOON-HO** in his 2019 Academy Awards acceptance
speech for Best Director (*Parasite*), quoting Martin Scorsese

The High Cost of Merely Surviving: The Problem with "Going Along to Get Along"

When I first started managing people, I never imagined that I could draw from my own early experiences growing up as a Korean American. Heck, I spent most of my time in the United States trying to reconcile the values I learned as a child with the American ones in the variety of spaces I existed. And the most difficult place to navigate that was in the corporate workplace.

In the beginning, I was busy trying to fit into a "white male model" of leading because that was what was rewarded and reinforced by my employers. It didn't occur to me to consider how the valuable early lessons learned from my community could possibly help me navigate the competitive workplace I found myself in.

For the majority of Asian Americans in my leadership coaching programs, their experiences are similar. When I start working with new clients, I often find that their mindset toward difference (which affects their interaction styles and approaches with non-Asian colleagues, including their managers) is right smack in the center of the intercultural development model—an important concept that I'll introduce soon. For now, though, just know that being in the middle means that on average, they're operating from a viewpoint of minimizing differences, where they are muting aspects of their identity in order to be accepted.

In other words, they're getting ahead at work and finding some success, but they're doing so by the "going along to get along" or "let's not make waves" method. They're not being intentional about how they demonstrate their value; rather, it's about survival. This also means that most are not having the courageous conversations with their colleagues or managers about their experiences. They're not sharing different insights about how to think about the business or how to drive their functions from a culturally diverse point of view.

Many individuals who participate in my team's programs have spent their first ten years in the workforce trying hard to be accepted by the dominant culture, emulating the "acceptable" leadership behaviors that are reinforced by their employers. And they have risen through the ranks to a certain point by following that playbook.

When I met with clients during and post-lockdown, many were close to burnout. Trying to get ahead in a space that didn't allow them to fully realize their authentic leadership voice was taking a toll. In one leadership program of thirty Asian Americans in a financial services organization, almost all of the leaders I met said, "This is what the organization is allowing me to be. I can't be an unapologetic 'culturally fluent leader' here because if I try to go outside of the lines, I'll get penalized. In this up-or-out culture, the company is definitely not ready to see leadership practiced in a different way."

As for me, it wasn't until I realized that I needed to embrace my differences that I learned how to become a culturally fluent leader. But first I needed to see and understand what those unique differences were.

Checkpoint

How about you? Are you able to bring attributes specific to your cultural experience (skills, knowledge, network, experiences, and ideas) to bear at your employer?

_____

If you did so, would they be affirmed?

_____

Is this an issue of concern for you?

_____

Why or why not?

_____

To tackle these issues, first I sat down and envisioned what I wanted my future leadership to look like so that I would have a clearly defined goal. After all, there's no _executing_ without first _assessing and planning_. In other words, we can't dive into applying or practicing leadership strategies when we haven't yet determined what type of future we're trying to create for ourselves or our employees. For example, when you picture yourself in the future, how have you transformed or grown in your leadership?

If we were working together, here are some questions that I might ask up front. Take some time to reflect on them a bit, as they will point to some critical aspects of your career development:

- What are some ways that you've integrated your cultural perspective into how you show up?

- What new conversations have you had with important stakeholders?

- How did you build trust with new colleagues or increase the depth of conversations within the relationships you already have?

In this first exercise, you'll encounter a few of the tools to help answer these questions. You can start naming the reality you'd like to create, break it down into parts in the coming year, and begin building the toolkit for your cultural deep-dive journey. Then, a follow-up exercise will help you begin to identify what you'll need to reach that destination. Time to get started!

 ## Envisioning Your Leadership Future

Let's start by envisioning what you want your leadership to look like a year from now.

Say I'm sitting down with you for a coffee break. It is _____ [current year +1]. Describe for me what you have accomplished in the past year.

Be as detailed as you can. Write down the names of individuals who have helped you as well as places you've been and family or friends who've supported you along the way.

Consider these guiding questions in forming your response:

- How have you developed in your leadership? How has your confidence level grown?

  _____

  _____

  _____

- What are some ways that you've integrated your cultural values and perspective more into how you show up for others? In the office? With your team members? With friends? In your community?

  _____

  _____

  _____

- What new conversations have you had with important stakeholders? What was different about those interactions? Who initiated the conversations?

  _____

  _____

  _____

- What did you do to strengthen your relationships at work and with stakeholders over the year? How did you build trust with new colleagues that you met? How did you deepen ongoing relationships?

Get as specific as you can. Name relationships you want to build from scratch and those you want to strengthen. Be aspirational: if there's someone you don't know and are really interested in meeting, write that person's name down too. Identify what interactions or experiences would help forge the trust with them.

_____

_____

_____

Your Story

1. What impact would you like to have made in your family?

_____

_____

2. Neighborhood or community?

_____

_____

3. With friends?

_____

_____

4. In your city? Your country?

_____

_____

5. In your industry?

_____

_____

6. What is currently missing in your life that you'd like to introduce?
(Stress-busting activities? More family time? A new exercise routine?
A better work/life integration?)

_____

_____

7. Fill in the blank:

I want to be viewed as _____.

Example: "I want to be viewed as an impactful leader who has made
critical contributions to the business, not just a reliable worker who's
good at getting things done. I'd like to be known by leaders in other
departments as someone who builds effective connections across conflicting divides and brings creativity to challenging business problems."

Now that you've done this work of imagining what you want your leadership to look like a year from now (with all the wisdom and experience gained from it), it's time to consider the ideal conditions that you will need in order to create that reality.

Those of you familiar with *Breaking the Bamboo Ceiling* may recall completing the forty-year vision activity. It involves a future look into how you want to be living your life, five years at a time. Even if you've completed it in the past, it's a good idea to revisit the vision every few years as circumstances in your life change. This activity builds on that exercise to help you envision your future in a more culturally integrated way.

Bringing Your Full Self to Leadership— Becoming an Integrated Leader

Ben Hires is CEO of the Boston Chinatown Neighborhood Center (BCNC), one of the leading nonprofit social service agencies for Asian and new immigrants in Boston (with sixty-five full-time and thirty-five part-time staff), providing childcare programs, education and workforce initiatives, family and community engagement opportunities, and arts and culture programs. Ben, a Korean American adoptee, is the first non-Chinese leader to head BCNC. Growing up in a rural town in New Jersey, he didn't know anyone in his neighborhood who looked like him. He recalls: "I've had to learn about the history of Boston's Chinatown and understand the Chinese immigration experiences, including that of my team; many of our staff members are bilingual and immigrants, and English is not their first language."

On top of that, while Ben looks Korean on the outside, his early cultural experience was different from that of his peers in college who grew up with Asian parents. "I look Asian, but because I was raised in a white family, I wasn't steeped in these Asian values, and now I find myself working for an organization who's working toward supporting the Chinese immigrant experience in the US."

Ben was director of strategic partnerships at Boston Public Library when his friend Giles Li, who was then the CEO of BCNC, decided to move to his next leadership role. Ben's name was frequently brought up for the role because of his experience working in the nonprofit space in the greater Boston area and the external perspective he could bring to the team. He came with no preconceived notions and no baggage. He started the job at BCNC in June 2020, a week or so after George Floyd was murdered, and he wrote the organization's first statement on racial justice. At the time, BCNC as an organization didn't have the fluency or racial justice framework to process this crisis, and didn't have a formal public position on racism or official processes to handle the hate incidents faced by Asian community members. Ben remembers, "All of this catalyzed embarking on our own racial justice journey. I discovered we were all on different pages about how BCNC should or shouldn't respond to these different scenarios."

During the pandemic, people stopped frequenting the restaurants and visiting the businesses in the Chinatown area. Business owners had a tremendous amount of fear and worry about losing their livelihood. As a result, BCNC collaboratively launched We Love Boston Chinatown, a resilience campaign to counter prejudice against Asians. As part of its efforts, the campaign put posters in the windows of local restaurants to increase their visibility.

As an outsider to the Chinese community, Ben has been instrumental in helping to build bridges with other ethnic communities. BCNC has had three strong years since Ben started and is on solid footing from a funding perspective. However, getting there wasn't as easy as it might sound. As a self-professed introvert, Ben had to work out of his comfort zone in order to take on fundraising. But with practice and after seeing success from his gradual efforts, he did it, which he admits "was very challenging for me, but it was necessary and now it's like old hat." His multicultural lens has helped him think out of the box and forge partnerships in the city that the organization had previously lacked. Eventually, additional funding came as a result of these relationships.

Describing his personal philosophy about leadership, Ben says, "I believe in leading with one's values. I believe in trusting one's gut or heart center, which is connected to the mind. I think I lead with vision and transformation in mind, and a focus on data and transparent information. I want to ensure our staff is happy and proud to work at BCNC and every person has what they need and the opportunity to become their best professional selves—that is what will allow for the biggest impact on our community."

In 2016, at the suggestion of his mentor, David Howse, who created a network of Black leaders, Ben serendipitously started an Asian American leadership group with Giles, his BCNC predecessor, to create an "A-team" to support Asian leaders in Boston. He recognizes the need to join forces to solve the city's toughest problems, since it won't be only one organization that will be able to solve them.

Defining Your Ideal Conditions: What Do You Need to Get There?

What resources, skills, or conditions do you need to reach your goals?

1. If you had no restrictions and an environment that would help you do your best work, what would that look like?

Check all that apply or add specifics that aren't listed.

☐ Great rapport with my manager

☐ Opportunity to work on a visible, cross-functional project

☐ Financial stability of the company

☐ Recognition for my contributions

☐ Variety in day-to-day work functions

☐ Access to support and resources

☐ Adequate agency to get things done

☐ Political air cover

☐ Competitive pay and benefits

☐ A sense of camaraderie with coworkers

☐ Good balance of work life and home life (e.g., vacation time)

☐ Inclusive and culturally aware management

☐ Flexibility in my workday (mix of in-person and virtual, ideal work hours, etc.)

☐ Culture that allows me to voice my opinions and concerns without fear of reprimand

Other _____

Other _____

Other _____

Your circle of support

2. Who will help you get there? Name them.

Family member(s)   _____

Friend(s)   _____

Co-worker(s)   _____

Manager(s)   _____

Client(s)   _____

Spouse/partner   _____

Vendor(s)/supplier(s)   _____

Anyone else? (This is your chance to go deeper.)

_____

_____

_____

3. What behaviors, tendencies, or attitudes in yourself did you have to eliminate in order to achieve your ideal working conditions within the year? And what attitudes or skills did you have to add?

_____

_____

_____

As you've seen from these exercises, by identifying our goals and the ideal conditions necessary for realizing them, we can be specific about what action steps we need to take. It's important to name and picture a future state that you're excited about since you'll be investing your time and energy into working toward that new future.

What would make a meaningful difference in helping you become a more effective, authentic, and valued leader—one who people are excited to work with and whose vision they want to rally around?

To answer this effectively, the first step is to dig deep to identify experiences you might have forgotten about or perhaps suppressed. At some distance, they might provide insight into aspects of your experience that need to be recognized, reconsidered, and better understood. This will involve unpacking the various aspects of your identity (such as your cultural values and practices, pivotal life moments, parents' experience, or birth order) that play a role in how you interact, communicate, and demonstrate your leadership every day. I recognize that not everything about your family or life experience might have been "positive" or "healthy." The point is that your life story can form the basis of your leadership story, and I'd like you to start thinking about how the learnings from those experiences might enhance your leadership going forward.

In the next chapter, you'll begin this process of diving into your cultural formation story. This will include exploring how you understand those experiences by unpacking cultural dimensions and communication styles. You might discover specific cultural perspectives that could be utilized to your advantage.

For now, though, take confidence from having identified your vision and your available resources. When taking a developmental approach to crafting your leadership style, you have to begin exactly where you are.

4

UNEARTHING YOUR IDENTITY

Digging Deeper and Knowing What You Offer

For someone who has spent years covering and hiding who I am, it's a slow process of peeling off the layers of protective armor.

—DAVID MOORE, production designer, Hallmark Cards

Unpacking the Elements of Your Identity

'm excited that you're open to exploring the cultural aspects of your identity and digging further into how they've shaped you. If you've come this far, you're ready to dig even deeper.

First, let's unpack the idea of culture in general. Very simply, culture is the shared beliefs and values of a group of people. How do you begin to define it? What makes you align with one preference over another? Do you take your shoes off in the house? Prefer rice over bread? Or bow whenever you visit your family members in Asia? All of those behaviors can be an indicator of cultural norms you've been socialized with. But culture doesn't just exist on the surface.

There are deeper cultural values that affect how we interact with each other that are reinforced by our communities. If you grew up in a family that values filial piety (reverence for one's elders), for example, your parents might think twice about putting your grandmother in a nursing home.

While culture is constantly shaping our behaviors, it's often unconscious to us and we're not always aware of its effects. If we live and work only with people like us, we might not always recognize our culturally learned behaviors. Or if we're working in a setting where our held values are in direct conflict with our corporate culture, we might intentionally suppress them in order to fit in or we might be discouraged from fully expressing them.

When we interact with people with unfamiliar values, preferences, or approaches, however, we start to notice the prevalence of culture. The complexity of the global, interconnected workplace can amplify misunderstandings, making it easy for underlying cultural values to collide. It takes a certain level of self-awareness to realize how your learned behavior affects the way you present yourself and interact with others. Therefore, in order to thrive as an effective leader operating in a multicultural workplace, you'll find it helpful to understand and name how culture has affected you specifically.

In this chapter, you'll explore the six dimensions of culture and start to name how they show up in your own leadership persona. You'll also learn about your preferred communication and conflict style. Throughout the chapter, I'll introduce you to Asian leaders who have learned through their own pivotal experiences (sometimes by surprise, and sometimes painfully) and have done the hard work of understanding how culture has affected their behavior and perceptions of others. By the end of this chapter, you'll have a deeper grasp of how your own experiences have shaped your actions—and how you can begin to use that knowledge as an asset in refining your own unique leadership style.

Culture: The Software of the Mind

Culture is anything that is expected and reinforced by a social group. When individuals from different social groups and communities start engaging, there's naturally a collision of values, norms, and expectations.

Like software, culture has an outward interface as well as a deeper core. Social psychologist Geert Hofstede describes culture as the mental programming of the mind. He says that by adolescence, these values are deeply instilled in us by our families and communities. Of course, through lived experiences outside of our cultural communities we learn to make adaptations, but those early "wirings" are deeply embedded. Some have even been there, unexamined, since childhood. And because everyone brings their own set of norms, preferences, and "default" behaviors to their interactions, engaging with new people can be even more complicated. Before we can skillfully address any new issues that might surface, we must untangle our cultural values. This begins with intentionally questioning our assumptions, and thereby becoming more capable of leveraging a multicultural perspective in the workplace.

You can think of culture as an iceberg. Eighty-five percent of it is submerged under the surface. The external, "above the waterline" aspects of culture (what I'll call the "visible" culture) include things like food, dance, music, art, and language. The internal, "below the waterline" aspects of culture ("invisible" culture) are more difficult to understand; often, they are not conspicuous to a person from outside that culture. Therefore, the implicit "rules" of a culture take some effort for an outsider to see and understand.

Revisiting Your Roots to Refine Your Leadership Voice

Mino Tsumura is the West Region Accounting and Reporting Advisory Leader for Deloitte. Throughout his life, Mino, a Japanese American, has had to adapt to many different cultural environments. Born in the United States, he took an opportunity from Deloitte to move to Tokyo for what turned into a five-year stint with a local team.

As he recalls: "Before I landed in Japan, I thought I had a good understanding of the Japanese culture and assumed my work skills and knowledge would translate to being a good manager in Japan. When I arrived in Japan, I quickly learned that the staff was overworked, seemed depressed, and was in a downward spiral of working long hours, waking up late, and falling asleep at their desks. It was a horrible work/life balance in Tokyo. I thought I would be able to lead them differently with work/life balance concepts from the US and help them see what I assumed was a better life. I was *wrong*.

"The mentality of people in Japan—their view toward work—is completely different from the US. They want to be working late, not necessarily to be productive but because it is almost a badge of honor to work long hours. The consensus-building culture and group mindset/collectivism further drove the long hours. Underlying everything is the idea that it's embarrassing to make mistakes and there is a constant drive for perfection.

"My assumption that I could have a huge impact on that team meant forcing the American way on a population that wasn't ready to, or didn't want to, adopt it. Consensus building is a process and a method for not making mistakes. The US likes to move at 1,000 miles per hour and is fine to make mistakes along the way. In Japan, it's more important to grow slowly with little or no mistakes along the way."

It was an adjustment for Mino to realize the subtleties of being in a country where, on the surface, he looked like many of its people, but he still felt disconnected from the people at times. Reflecting on his time in Japan, Mino said, "I don't think they planned on me asking them to do all the things I did, like asking them to consider working differently. They probably expected me to fit in and just work with them. I speak Japanese and understand the language pretty well, so they treated me a little differently than they would treat other foreigners. I was also in the field working alongside them on assignments, which was different than the other expatriates who came to Japan and were not allowed to have direct client interactions. Even so, they saw me as different from them—I was Japanese American, and they would call me a *nisei* (second generation) or foreigner."

Using the skills of observation, bridging, inquiry, and learning from his earlier missteps has helped Mino flex his cultural fluency muscle effectively while engaging his new global management responsibilities. For Mino, being thrust into a different national culture helped him understand how his own cultural upbringing shaped his understanding of the world, and this became the catalyst that drove him to refine his intercultural leadership skills. In the next activity, see if you can frame your own workplace experience by learning from the visible and invisible cultural examples you recognize from Mino's story.

 ## Understanding Culture

1. Next to the graphic, write out three examples of visible aspects of your own culture. Be as specific as you want to be. (Examples: speaking Hindi and English fluently, using honorific language with elders, celebrating certain holidays.)

2. Next, write out three less visible examples of your own culture below the waterline. What are some deeply ingrained cultural values or beliefs that you grew up with? (Example: being taught to think about others in the group and not just yourself.)

3. What behaviors do you demonstrate that might be an indicator of deeper cultural values that are underneath the waterline? (Example: being great at reading the room because you're attuned to how indirect and nonverbal communication styles were used in your family.)

Understanding Culture—Iceberg Graphic Organizer

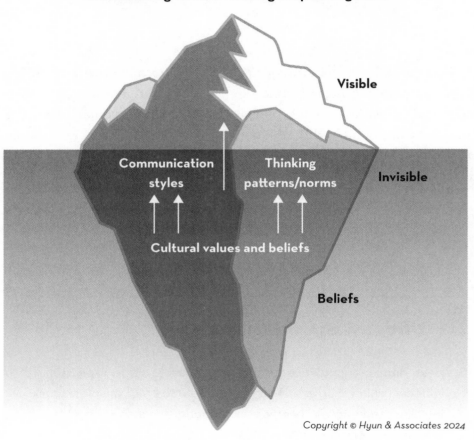

Communication styles

Thinking patterns/norms

Visible

Invisible

Cultural values and beliefs

Beliefs

Copyright © Hyun & Associates 2024

Becoming Aware of Difference

Jenny Lee, the vice president of Global Digital Marketing and Customer Experience at Boston Scientific, first realized she was different in elementary school. She recalls, "One day, on the bus, a student came up to me and in a very negative tone said, 'How come you don't have any eyelashes?'" At the time, Jenny hadn't realized there was anything separating her from her peers. "It didn't make sense to me," she says, "because I didn't know my eyes were different. I went home and I started to talk with my parents about it. My being different became very clear, and also the impact that it had on the people around me."

Because Asians grow up steeped in their culture from a young age, there's often a clear moment when they realize that their cultural norms are not the same as those around them. For example, maybe you recall asking friends visiting your home to take their shoes off—a behavior that was automatic to you. Or maybe, as in Jenny's experience, others picked up on these differences before you did—which then led to critical comments and, ultimately, changing your behavior to avoid the unpleasantness of being ostracized. You were dealing with the harsh realization that you had to minimize parts of yourself in order to fit into the dominant culture around you.

 ## When Was the First Time You Became Aware That You Were Different?

Reflecting on your life, when was the first time you realized that you were somewhat different from your classmates or peers?

_____

How has that difference affected you in your workplace?

_____

Do your colleagues know your heritage, experience, or cultural story?

_____

In what ways might you downplay aspects of your background or differences?

_____

The Challenge: Getting Past Minimizing Differences

You might have already spent the first half of your career trying to excel by being accepted by the dominant culture. But what if, instead of trying to be accepted, you leaned into more of who you are? There are aspects of your cultural experience that are valuable, and by deeply grounding yourself in who you are and leaning into your cultural story, you'll discover how you can use your lived experiences to be a more holistic leader. In the next chapter, we'll explore more of how your mindset toward cultural difference could be of value to you. After all, mindset will affect how successful you will be in implementing these tools. But for now, it's important to recognize that your cultural experience impacts you in both positive and negative ways.

In my team's leadership programs, we often discuss the importance of understanding the impact of _minimization_ in the workplace. What I mean by that is that sometimes Asians are not aware of how much they're adapting to fit into a dominant culture. They _diminish_ or _minimize_ themselves so as to not make waves or in order to adapt to what they see as "successful."

My own form of downplaying my experience happened early in my career, when I attempted to hide my differences from my colleagues. I never talked about my personal life or the distinctly "Korean American" activities I participated in outside of work. I rarely referred to the leadership roles I played in the Asian American community, whether it was in my church, volunteering at ethnic-specific mentoring organizations, or community groups. I connected with my white coworkers on a level that they could understand, which meant focusing on what we had in common with less emphasis on the distinctive aspects of myself. So, I had this alternative life outside of work where I was influencing, practicing my leadership, and giving back to my community that no one really outside of my Asian American circle could appreciate. It took me a while to feel comfortable relating to them in a way that brought them into my cultural experience, since it just sounded so out of the mainstream at the time. If you've been doing this, know that I see you. And I will help you identify ways to use your experiences creatively throughout this book—no experience will be wasted!

We each bring unique points of view to our companies. Consequently, gaining greater cultural self-awareness is critical to defining your own leadership approach. The first step you can take to achieve personal growth is exploring your cultural values.

Over time, I realized that no matter how different I am from others, I could still find points of connection by bridging through commonality or difference. It's those points that then allowed me to open up about my differences and eventually helped me stop downplaying my own cultural aspects in order to fit into the dominant culture. But that had to start with me and my journey of embracing my culture (the good and the bad) and creating meaning out of my own identity.

Gaining greater cultural self-awareness is critical to defining your own leadership approach. The first step you can take to achieve personal growth is exploring your cultural values.

How has your culture shaped you, and what can that tell you about your own differences?

The Dimensions of Culture

To unpack your own cultural experiences, you must first understand how culture has impacted your life. What were you raised to believe about the world?

How did that affect your notion of what's the right way to behave and what's not? What was rewarded and reinforced?

Engineer and Dutch social psychologist Geert Hofstede conducted primary field research that led him to develop a six-dimensional model that explores how culture manifests in societies and organizations. Hofstede has continued to develop this research-based framework over the years, and his six dimensions—individualism, power distance, certainty, time, achievement, and indulgence—are very useful for helping individuals and organizations navigate a rapidly globalizing world. How you answer the questions in Hofstede's model can help determine what you value and how it affects the way you show up in the workplace. As an example, because of the way you were socialized and brought up, you might have a tendency to avoid challenging people who are older or in positions of authority. That doesn't mean you do this in every interaction, but this is your tendency. This is what Hofstede calls a *hierarchical orientation* with respect to the power distance dimension. In an organizational setting in a high-power-distance culture, subordinates likely expect more direction from their management; in an organization with more participative or egalitarian orientation, however, subordinates would take more initiative with their managers and are comfortable expressing a contrary point of view.

By starting to look at your own life experiences through the critical dimensions of culture, you can learn a lot about the values instilled in you from a young age and what that means for your current behavior. Below, I've broken down each dimension, along with the extreme orientations, to help you determine where you might fall in a broad sense. Please note that this is simply an overview—in our assessment work, my team and I bring in the Hofstede Culture in the Workplace Questionnaire™ (CWQ) to better understand cultural dimensions on a deeper level. This helps us connect the impact of your family experiences with the way that you respond to others in the workplace. For now, as you read, I encourage you to evaluate your own experiences to see if you're closer to one orientation or the other.[1]

---

[1] These definitions of the six dimensions are adapted from Hofstede's Culture in the Workplace Questionnaire™. Reach out to us at *info@hyunassociates.com* if you'd like to take it with your team.

Understanding the Dimensions of Culture

Individualism (individual or group)

The degree to which action is taken for the benefit of the individual or the group.

Individual ◄————————————► Group

Add your own example of how this preference shows up in your life:

_____

_____

Power distance (hierarchical or egalitarian/participative)

The amount of social distance you place between yourself and those in positions of authority; how you navigate status differences.

Hierarchical ◄————————————► Egalitarian

Your example:

_____

_____

Certainty (need for certainty or tolerance for ambiguity)

The extent to which you prefer rules, regulations, and controls, or are more comfortable with unstructured or unpredictable situations.

Need for certainty ←————————————————→ Tolerance for ambiguity

Your example:

_____

_____

Time (short term or long term)

The extent to which you either are prepared to adapt yourself in the long term in order to attain a desirable future or prefer to take guidance from the past and focus on fulfilling present needs.

Short term ←————————————————→ Long term

Your example:

_____

_____

Achievement (quality of life or achievement)

The degree to which you focus on goal achievement and work or quality of life and caring for others.

Achievement ←————————————————→ Quality of life

Your example:

_____

_____

Indulgence (indulgence or restraint)

The tendency to focus on enjoying life, well-being, and being happy, or the conviction that gratification needs to be regulated by strict social norms.

Indulgence ←——————————————→ Restraint

Your example:

_____

_____

Mino's perspective (from his leadership story earlier in the chapter) can be helpful in showing how these six dimensions help to shape cultural values. For example, his experience demonstrated the high need for certainty in his Tokyo office. He shares: "When I was in Japan, there was a point when I couldn't understand why the local audit staff and managers didn't want to be fast or efficient. What it came down to was a sense of perfection . . . it is deeply ingrained over there; people don't want to make mistakes. High quality is extremely valued and I didn't fully appreciate that until I was there. From my perspective, I thought it was slow, inefficient [at first]. When you sit and live and breathe it, that high quality ingrained in everything you do is the driver for how they operate."

Which cultural dimension(s) took you by surprise? What can it tell you about your own cultural experience?

_____

For me, it was power distance that brought continued tension into my professional life. In the introduction to this book, I mentioned moving to New York City in the third grade from Korea and coming head-to-head with a very egalitarian classroom. I went from a place where obedience and silence in the classroom were expected, to being rewarded for speaking up and openly debating with the teacher. I felt this power distance disconnect immediately, though I couldn't name it at the time. Additionally, Americans, being focused on individual expression and independence, were more outspoken than anyone I had experienced in Korea.

After you work through this book, I encourage you to take the CWQ. This instrument shows your cultural dimension preference relative to how different national cultures have scored, which is a useful way to show how your individual preferences compare to a variety of national cultures. If you're working in a multicultural setting or a global team, having this knowledge can enable you to be proactive about ways to work more effectively together, or at a minimum, give you a basis for an onboarding conversation with a new team—allowing you go in with eyes wide open about potential areas of difference. This is why cultural dimensions can be so important to know: they help provide context for how and why you're showing up in your workplace. That self-awareness is often the first step in becoming a strong leader, since leadership is all about working with others to get objectives accomplished, right?

Navigating Diverse Communication and Conflict Styles

Another area where culture plays a central role is in communication and conflict styles. For example, when doing a project with the local office in Turkey, an American leader once called out a local office employee and spoke in detail about what he needed to do differently. That direct callout created tremendous tension in an environment where a more indirect cultural communication style was the norm, and it was difficult for the meeting to recover. If we are socialized with a different style of navigating difficult situations, we may shut down and refuse to engage.

Consider these two questions when you are working in multicultural work settings:

- Are we able to *truly* hear the other party's perspective and the message that the other party is intending to convey?

- What conflicts might arise simply due to misunderstandings in intercultural communication styles?

Depending on your cultural background, you will approach communication through a specific lens. And if you're interacting with someone who has a completely different communication style, your approach could help resolve or amplify a conflict situation; it all depends on whom you're interacting with.

In cultures that have a *direct* communication style, you'll see precise use of language, reasoned arguments, and a problem/solution orientation. Words will be used as a focal point to communicate a message. In cultures with an *indirect* style, language is more ambiguous and there's more of a focus on repairing and preserving harmony in the relationship. They might use nonverbal cues, like a change in eye contact, body language, tone of voice, or use of metaphors, to indicate their approval or disapproval. Both of these styles have their strengths and challenges, and it's important to note that one approach may not always work in every situation, and both are valid ways to resolve conflict.

When working with different styles, you can't expect those with an opposing style to meet you where you are. Ideally, both parties should mutually attempt to adapt to each other's style. In the absence of that, leading with an attitude of humility and a willingness to meet them partway may result in a more productive work relationship.

Embracing Differences to Become a Bridge Builder

The importance of navigating different communication styles is something that Korean American Marshall Cho, who recently completed a stint as head basketball coach at Lake Oswego High School, knows well. Recruited out of college to join the prestigious Teach for America program, his first assignment placed him as a math teacher in a classroom in the South Bronx. When he walked in on the first day of school and started to take attendance, two female students stood up and declared, "Oh, hell no! Not this guy!" and proceeded to walk out of the classroom. At that point, something instinctive kicked in for Marshall and he recalled the values he learned in South Korea about how you should never disrespect the teacher. In Korea, you would start each day standing up with the classroom officer and say together in unison, "Thank you for teaching us today" to show respect to the teacher. He could not believe that the students would dare walk out on him in the first five minutes of his teaching career.

As the girls started to walk away, Marshall took the clipboard he was holding and slapped it against the desk, inadvertently breaking it in half. At this, the two girls stopped and looked at him, and then backpedaled to their seats. After completing the roll call, he proceeded to teach the class.

Not only is this an example of power distance—showing how we can be socialized to understand conceptions of power in different ways—but it's also an example of how different communication styles can be perceived in a cross-cultural environment. In this case, that direct, expressive style worked: the students returned to class and grew to respect Marshall as a teacher because he exerted his authority in the classroom with strong expressiveness. In addition to directness, your communication and conflict style can be emotionally expressive or restrained—and each approach might work in different settings.

The fundamental cultural elements that affect communication and conflict styles are how directly or indirectly you discuss problems and conflicts and how you express emotion around them. The trick is to recognize what your style is and how it manifests when you're dealing with individuals whose style differs from yours.

In addition to understanding your cultural preferences as well as other conflict and communication styles as you refine your leadership, part of defining your own leadership approach entails knowing how to engage around those differences. This involves being able to have a dialogue about your cultural preferences with others and negotiating the different styles that you will encounter in the workplace so that you can better grasp the meaning behind your colleagues' actions and create shared meaning.

Seeing and Acknowledging Difference

I've embraced being different, and
that's what has allowed me to be successful.

—MARSHALL CHO

As Marshall showed through his teaching, difference isn't always a bad thing; often, it's what can help us create a bridge toward understanding one another. By approaching his students in a new way (that drew on his personal experiences), he was able to connect with them. This continued throughout his teaching career, and word got around that if you disrespected Mr. Cho, he would pay you a visit at home. He also used basketball as a connector. He would go out into the field and play basketball with the students. He was good, and the kids took notice. When the kids came back into the classroom after watching him play, they would say, "Mr. Cho has game!" He ended up teaching at the same school for six more successful years, and he says that it helped him learn to meet people where they're at: "Being an immigrant, I knew what it meant to be an outsider and how to build bridges. I knew how to do that."

Marshall is the perfect example of how important it is to understand your values and use them to your advantage in order to create the kind of relational connections that lead to a more productive workplace. Part III will talk more about what it means to move to a more culturally fluent place where you can leverage these differences for your growth and career advancement. For now, I want you to start thinking about the ways that your differences have shaped you—and to acknowledge that those experiences can be valuable when it comes to increasing your cultural self-awareness.

Becoming More Grounded in Your Cultural Identity

To become more culturally grounded, you need to combine cultural self-aware-ness with mindfulness about the differences that others bring. How do you better understand and ground yourself in your cultural experience instead of running away from it or exerting energy trying to fit in with the dominant culture? What do you need to declare—to both the people who care about your development and your organization—in order to be more authentic in your workplace?

As you continue to explore aspects of your experience and seek to culturally ground yourself, you'll start to see new aspects of your hidden "assets" emerge. And you'll see that what was once perhaps a difference that annoyed you or that you tried to suppress can now be put to use as an important leadership tool. Over time, you might even find that you can unearth a unique skill that you can leverage as a leader.

Delving Deeper to Find Your Authentic Voice

Years ago, when someone gave me my own assessment to gauge my cultural flu-ency, I wasn't sure what to expect. But when the results came back and I discov-ered that I was not as far along as I thought, I was shocked! How could I have overestimated my own abilities? I was already doing leadership development with an inclusive lens and talking about culture, so how could I still have some feelings of judgment against my own cultural values? After I cooled down, I took a cold hard look at how I was showing up in the office. I started to see how I was talking about leadership but not actually leaning into how my personal experiences had shaped my strengths as a leader—oftentimes without realizing it.

But becoming aware of this transformed how I look at leadership and motivated me to help others learn how to change their mindsets. For the past nineteen years, I've focused on helping others become effective at leading across differences in increasingly global organizations where bridging cultural differences (without burning bridges or breaking relationships) is a critical skillset.

To make that fundamental change, I needed to dig deep and to find my authentic voice—which meant leaving behind the Minimization mindset I had developed. (Chapter 5 will explore the mindsets with which people approach difference.) You might not have spent a lot of time focusing on your authentic voice yet, instead hiding your cultural attributes or code switching in order to cope. But the more authentic and "real" you can be without hiding yourself, the more successful you'll become in the long run.

The Cost of "Going Along"

I once facilitated a panel discussion with a Black female executive who told me she spent twelve years of her career straightening her hair and toning down her voice so as not to appear too loud or expressive. She was avoiding being seen as different, because she didn't want to be pigeonholed with the "angry Black woman" stereotype. Hiding herself in this way caused a tremendous amount of stress and pressure in her life, and it required an additional level of exertion that was hard to sustain. Additionally, there were times when she held back from sharing a different point of view because she was so used to editing herself at work. When she moved into a midlevel position, she finally became more comfortable showing her true self—and this led to her achieving more at work and engaging in deeper conversations with her colleagues. It was in allowing her authentic self to shine that she realized her own strength as a leader. When the right conditions are present, difference can be an asset that can help you become the leader you're meant to be. By not hiding yourself, you're better able to share your unique perspective and to contribute in more productive ways.

Throughout this chapter, we've explored the dimensions of culture and how it can affect your own behaviors in the workplace. We've looked at how communication and conflict styles can vary and potentially escalate disagreements when cultural differences are ignored. Most importantly, we've discussed how difference can become an asset in the workplace and how a shift in your mindset can help you become culturally grounded. The next step is to start examining how you actively engage with difference and how all the parts of yourself—your culture, your personality, your background—could potentially contribute to your authentic voice as a leader. As you continue to navigate a global workplace, the right mindset toward difference is everything.

Key Learning Points

- Culture exists in virtually every human interaction, and it can show up in visible and invisible ways. As with an iceberg, there is much below the surface, so when in doubt, expect that there are differences at play.

- Hofstede's six dimensions of culture is a framework that sheds light on the cultural differences that exist in the workplace. This model provides a common language for building your cultural self-awareness and cultural other-awareness.

- When you lean into your cultural identity and better understand your experience, you can see your unique perspectives clearly and transform differences into potential strengths.

- Digging deeper to unearth your authentic voice is key to becoming an effective leader. What have you learned from your personal experiences? Can you identify pivotal life-shaping moments that have informed your approach to leadership and how you might grow moving forward?

5

HOW DO YOU ENGAGE WITH DIVERSITY AND DIFFERENCE?

Understanding culture is the foundation . . . it is the most difficult concept to find widespread agreement on, yet it is central to everything.

—MITCHELL HAMMER, PhD, founder of IDI, LLC; author; and professor emeritus of International Peace and Conflict Resolution, American University

Once I was able to internalize my starting point in Minimization and stopped fighting the development process I needed to go on, I was able to advance my journey forward. I took ownership over it!

—VEENA LAKKUNDI, global business leader

n the last chapter, you began thinking about how your own experience living in different cultural environments has shaped you. In this one, we'll be diving deeper into how you respond to difference when you're faced with it in the workplace or in your community.

Identifying Your Starting Point

Your mindset toward difference informs everything about how you work with others, and your attitude toward people who are not like you. How does that manifest for you? Do you try to ignore difference because you're afraid of dealing with or talking about it? Is it hard to even know where to start? Or are you able to adapt your practices in the moment when you realize something's not working? Knowing how you respond will determine how ready you are to adopt some of the new learnings throughout this book. Being able to discern complexity and engage effectively with people who are not like you will become increasingly important as you move up the leadership ranks. If you're not yet where you'd like to be, continually working on your mindset as you refine your leadership approach and put new skills into practice will help you start to respond to difference in a healthy way.

We are all on a path of discovery, and it's important that we lead with *compassion* for where others are on that journey as we interact with them. I want to underscore that there's no judgment for wherever you find yourself in this journey—whether you're fully aware of how culture has affected you or this is the first time you've thought about it. By choosing to go down this path, you're making a conscious decision to discover what makes you who you are and how that can affect the ways in which you work with others.

One reason that many leadership initiatives underperform when they involve diverse, multicultural work teams is because they don't recognize that, as leaders, we may need to use different strategies to engage with individuals who are from diverse backgrounds and therefore have different preferences and communication styles. Most leaders I begin working with are accustomed to using the same approaches for everyone—a one-size-fits-all attitude. Hence, the way they build trust, make decisions, and resolve challenges doesn't always work for everyone involved. Add in a multicultural, global perspective, and this attitude creates even more room for misunderstandings and barriers to true collaboration. Operating from a one-size-fits-all approach in a multicultural work setting increases the risk of making costly mistakes.

As you lead, you will be influencing, motivating, and engaging the various people in your "ecosystem." That includes your direct reports, peers in other business groups, manager, senior management (and matrix bosses), customers, and suppliers or vendors. Because intercultural skills in leadership—or cultural fluency—are the "how" of connecting the dots within a diverse workforce, they're crucial. If you have cultural fluency in your toolkit, you'll be more likely to create an environment that ensures people feel valued and engaged enough to contribute. Thus, before you learn more advanced leadership concepts, it's important to get a sense of where you currently are in your cultural fluency.

The Intercultural Development Continuum© and the Path to Cultural Fluency

After my keynote presentation on culturally fluent leadership principles, a CEO approached me. He told me how excited he was about what I had just presented on and wanted to share his own philosophy about leading. He said that no matter who he was talking to, no matter what their background was, his leadership mantra was about putting this "golden rule" into practice with all of his global offices (the company had a significant presence throughout Europe, Asia, and Africa): "My leadership philosophy is centered around respect."

While I understood and valued his response, I had also been working with the head of HR and diversity leader and knew that his organization often operated from the mindset of *Minimization*—that is, they didn't always talk about differences and there was general anxiety about bringing up differences across culture, ethnicity, or race. There was a tendency to "standardize" the new programs and products they implemented

"My leadership philosophy is centered around respect."

around the globe. After hearing the CEO's philosophy, I paused for a moment and then responded with: "Respect is absolutely critical. I'm glad to hear that your leadership approach starts with your desire to honor others. How might the folks across all the diverse groups we talked about interpret how you show that respect? Could it differ from time to time?" My inquiry was meant to push his thinking further while keeping him engaged, because the implication he was making was that respect is a universal value. I wanted him and his leadership team to see beyond that, to explore how respect might look to people who interpret that core leadership value differently and to understand that cultural context could play a role. Many leaders use words like *respect* and *integrity* liberally, without thinking through how they land or are interpreted by a multicultural or global audience.

Context is crucial, but it can often be hard to see—especially within ourselves. Thankfully, we have the Intercultural Development Inventory® (IDI), a tool that measures where we fall along the Intercultural Development Continuum (IDC©) (see figure 5-1). Based on the Developmental Model of Intercultural Sensitivity (DMIS), the IDC model was developed by Dr. Mitchell Hammer and has been used by thousands of organizations to perform assessments or audits to determine the most useful next steps for their leadership

Intercultural Development Continuum

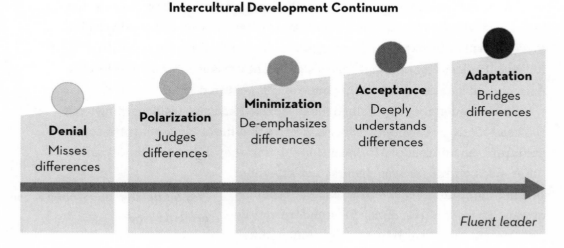

Source: Hyun & Associates, based on M. R. Hammer's Intercultural Development Continuum (https://www.idiinventory.com/idc), adapted from M. Bennett's Developmental Model of Intercultural Sensitivity (DMIS). Fluent leader stages excerpted from J. Hyun and A. Lee, *Flex: The New Playbook for Managing across Differences* (HarperCollins Business, 2014).

FIGURE 5-1. The path to cultural fluency

coaching efforts. On your own path of understanding your mindset toward difference and becoming culturally fluent, the IDI can be a very useful tool to get a sense of where you're starting out—and where you'd like to ultimately end up.

Personally, I have found the IDC useful when I'm assessing leadership teams and executive boards or when I'm working with people who are trying to manage a diverse, multicultural workforce. It allows me to develop the right type of training or coaching; I can design the intervention or teaching approach that would be most conducive to helping someone learn. In other words, I try to meet people where they are to ensure that they're *learning* from there. If a large percentage of the leaders in an organization are operating from a Polarization mindset—meaning they're judging people who are different from them and not trying to work with those differences at all—they're probably not ready to hear Adaptation strategies on day one.

I've seen firsthand the cost of not taking this into consideration. One client told me that right before she engaged my firm to teach cultural fluency skills to her management team, she had worked with a PhD who was an expert on cultural differences. Without doing any assessments, he went in and taught the team the main differences between the European heritage company and the Middle Eastern heritage company that had just completed a merger. The training initiative did not go well. It only created more of a rift in what was already a heated, judgmental atmosphere where there was finger-pointing and built-up tension on both sides. It did not result in greater understanding and increased collaboration among the leadership teams. My client was in repair mode when she contacted us.

In contrast to the PhD "expert," we used a developmental approach by assessing the employees with the IDI and led with a listening posture. We then created a customized program designed to address where they were. The results were more effective and the roundtable conversations were well received—even welcomed. We were able to help employees at the company see how their differences influenced their communication styles and to create a clear path forward to help them integrate more effectively—a path that didn't ignore the presence of culture in their work teams. This is why the assessment is so powerful: it gives you an honest sense of where you are in terms of cultural fluency, which in turn gives you a better understanding of what your next steps should be in leading from a multicultural perspective.

The Five Mindsets of the Developmental Model

Now that you understand *why* it's so important to assess your cultural fluency, let's break down the five stages of the IDC that show how you respond to difference when you encounter it. As you read, see if this language resonates with you so you can begin to gauge where you fall on this continuum.

- **Denial:** Do you avoid difference or actively withdraw from it?

    An individual in this mindset does not see differences in behavior as cultural. Difference is something to be avoided. When this mindset is prevalent in a leader, their employees can feel that diversity or difference is ignored.

- **Polarization:** Do you judge or evaluate difference? Do you see one culture's values and practices as better than another?

    This mindset can manifest in two ways. The first is defense, which means seeing another group's cultural values or practices as threatening to your own approaches and practices. The second is reversal, or idealizing another culture's values and practices while being overly critical of your own.

- **Minimization:** Do you value diversity and differences but tend to highlight commonalities rather than difference?

    An individual in this orientation tends to focus on what they have in common with others in a way that might mask recognition of deeper differences. They might focus on the fact that "people are people" and strive to find what they have in common with others. They may place an emphasis on universal values, such as the CEO who espoused respect (without interrogating what that meant). The urge to maintain the status quo and not "rock the boat" can be powerful.

If you find yourself in this mindset as an Asian American or another nondominant-culture identity group, it's not necessarily because you don't see the differences across cultures. Very often, it stems from a desire to get along with the dominant culture environment as a means of survival. You might think, *Talking about differences may not be appreciated here; it could backfire and affect my career progression.* People learn how to minimize differences in order to be accepted and to advance.

- **Acceptance:** Do you deeply see and understand differences in a way that makes you want to do something about it?

  In Acceptance, an individual can recognize difference and commonality in their own and other cultures. They are curious to learn how a pattern of behavior makes sense in other cultural groups and want to understand how they can work with those differences. However, they might not always know what to do about it.

- **Adaptation:** Do you adapt your behavior when needed and shift your mindset in appropriate ways?

  An individual in this mindset uses a wide repertoire of adaptive strategies to bridge differences. For example, they might say, "When we have conference calls with our counterparts in our offices in East Asia, I often adapt how I present my material for the clients in the region as they have other requirements."

A culturally fluent leader is someone who works very effectively with people who are different from them—and this creates an environment where their employees feel like they have a voice, leading to a more engaged and productive team culture overall.

Here are some reflection questions you might consider about the five mindsets of the model:

- What are the "mantras" that you use to work with others, whether you have verbalized them or not?

- Which of the five different mindsets of the model do you encounter most often in your work team? In your community?

- If you've already taken the IDI, were you surprised by your results? (If you're curious about the IDI and interested in taking it with your team, contact us at *info@hyunassociates.com*.)

A Global Strategy Leader's Cultural Fluency Journey

Veena Lakkundi, an Indian American, has been a global bridge builder throughout her career. Born in the United Kingdom and raised in Canada, she has led large teams in Asia and the United States and currently serves as the chief strategy officer for Rockwell Automation. Talking with Veena, I was immediately struck by the heartfelt enthusiasm that she brings to her work. She recounted to me how discovering her own "cultural mindset" made a tremendous difference in her approach to leading globally.

"When I got my IDI results, I thought to myself: How could this possibly be? I was already a diversity champion and had been leaning in to support corporate initiatives; I was hurt and humbled." At first, she felt that it was other people who needed to change. While that was also true, the more she reflected, the more she realized there were ways that she had to grow as well.

Part of the shock came from the fact that Veena speaks multiple languages and had already worked in a variety of cultures. If she was already so globally minded, how could she be in Minimization? But the IDC model is a reminder that your ability to navigate cultural differences doesn't improve merely from exposure to different cultural values and practices. You can't become culturally fluent by osmosis. It takes intentional work, reflection, and practice to move to a more multicultural orientation.

This was a critical leadership pivot point for Veena. She started to see her work differently and recognized that to be a more effective business leader she needed to take it to a more personal, intentional level. "Since then, I've internalized why I started out in Minimization, and I stopped fighting the development journey I had to go on. I realized I *wasn't* paying attention to my own unconscious biases, and I had to do that work. I owned it and took the journey forward!"

Veena took her development seriously while navigating her leadership. As she worked on deepening her own perspective and uncovering her biases, courageously delving further into her own cultural story, she became a more effective advocate for women and people of color. "I very much worked on it and got over the hump." And now she's in Acceptance—a more multicultural mindset.

"Today, I'm usually the one in the room where if there's a global initiative being discussed on a call, I'm asking if they have included the voices from X region or Y office, and if so, do they have a seat at the decision-making table? [Even if] it's a professional development program, it has to work from a truly global perspective in practice. And that goes for our employee side *and* the business side. On the business side, the voice of the customer truly has to be global, and not just in name."

To this day, Veena's strength comes from her ability to truly live out the values of the company while inspiring others to do the same. During the pandemic, she heard about the rise in incidents of violence against Asian women and it emboldened her to speak up on behalf of the AAPI community in her company, including becoming a sponsor for the Asian ERG. In every interaction, she brings a synergistic blend of direct communication style and a respectful air in how she conveys her message.

Moving Forward with Self-Compassion

As you can see, it's not enough to know what cultural values and preferences exist in your workplace. It's also important to gauge how you typically deal with diversity and difference so that you can determine what strategies will support your intercultural development. For example, if you find yourself in the Polarization mindset, you can start to recognize when you're evaluating the differences of a particular group of people without fully understanding them and then search for commonalities where you think none exist.

Veena's cultural journey showed me how important it was for her to realize how she was operating, even if she didn't like the results at first! More importantly, she resolved to do something about it and resisted the temptation to ignore the discomfort of discovering where she was actually operating from versus where she aspired to be as a leader. It's tempting to remain in your mindset, especially if your organization reinforces it by not encouraging a culture where you can speak up about differences. It's so easy to get comfortable and not move past the status quo. Differences make many of us uncomfortable. But Veena chose to close that gap between perception and reality, investing time and effort into increasing her understanding of her own cultural experience. At the same time, she sought to deepen her understanding of others, all with the goal of being more effective at engaging her teams.

We are all on our respective roads to discovery, so try to extend the same compassion to yourself as you do to others who are also learning. I want to underscore that there's no judgment for wherever you find yourself in this journey; it's where you decide to go from here that's more important.

Knowing her mindset acted like a GPS for Veena's future leadership development. She knew exactly what to tackle next as she considered how she could make the most impact in her leadership role. In thinking about your career objectives, how could knowing your mindset about diversity or difference help you identify your next steps? As you contemplate this, I encourage you to bring this level of openness into your own life, so that, like Veena, you can be honest about the mindset you're operating from when you encounter difference.

Application and Reflection

- What did you observe from Veena's story about her discovery of finding herself in the Minimization mindset?

- There are junctures in our careers when intent and impact don't align in our leadership. Describe a moment where your best intentions were not fully understood by others (i.e., when your intentions were misaligned with the impact they had). What did you do about it?

- Leadership is all about the how. When you work across differences, what aspects are easy for you? What is more challenging?

- Revisit the goal you set in chapter 1, where you envisioned what your leadership would look like one year from now. Knowing what you know now, is there anything you would change?

6

DESIGNING YOUR PERSONALIZED LEADERSHIP MODEL

When I dare to be powerful—to use my strength in the service of my vision—then it becomes less and less important whether I am afraid.

—AUDRE LORDE, writer, professor, and activist

Growing up, I was always intrigued by the Choose Your Own Adventure books. They allowed the reader to put themselves in the shoes of the main character (a spy, racecar driver, or mountain climber, for example) and then choose from a variety of options that determined how the story unfolded. Through those doors, I could wind up in one of many different endings. It was fascinating to see what would happen if I chose a different path or how the decisions I made would change the ending. I loved the concept that we, as young readers, were being asked the important questions: *What do you think will happen next? How can you determine the course of your future through your decisions?*

Similarly, you're now at the point in this book where you get to choose your own path forward. What kind of leader do you want to be? What experiences might you pursue to increase the skill sets you need to grow as a leader? Now that you have a stronger grasp of your vision, goals, and cultural values, you're ready to design a model for leadership that is unique to you. Consider this a Choose Your Own Adventure for your leadership future.

A Word about Leadership

There are many ways to think about leadership, and there's no consensus on what makes an effective leader. I've discovered that when you put together your own series of strategies and tools (maybe even create your own approaches) to lead and work with others, you'll have a greater likelihood of succeeding. Being bicultural, bilingual, and not easily fitting into any one leadership approach, I have consistently had to take the leadership concepts I was taught and figure out how to adapt and refine them so that they could work for *me*. By definition, I have had to *innovate* my own leadership style, through trial and error. For example, people often cite humility as a valuable quality in leaders, but this wasn't the case for me, and it isn't for many others, either.

Take William, a Chinese American leader in the financial services industry, who confided to me, "Well, the mantra 'Be humble' may work for the six foot two white guy who's perceived as confrontational, direct, and brash to show a dose of self-deprecation with his team—it allows his employees to see another side of him that others don't always see. But what if I'm naturally a reserved person [who's] really great at energizing people and great at getting people to achieve their best?" Doubling down on being modest and self-deprecating won't necessarily work well for an individual who is already riddled with the external perception that they're a "quiet, individual contributor."

In this case, William might benefit from emphasizing that his strength is in his uncanny ability to energize others with his innovative vision for the future and laser focus on mobilizing his team to achieve it. After all, leading people is about mobilizing others to action, not doing everything yourself. What does it matter that you're not as confrontational as the next person, as long as you are effective at getting results? But for anyone who has struggled with a variation of *imposter syndrome*—feeling inadequate when compared to others or worrying that someone will discover that you're not cut out for a job—grounding yourself in your own approach may validate the importance of your unique strengths while helping others see them too.

One Size Does *Not* Fit All

Whenever I think about alternative forms of leadership, my mind conjures up images of Neddy Perez, the chief diversity officer of McCormick. Neddy was always steadfast about her opinions, but in a thoughtful way. She had leadership presence and exuded confidence in a style all her own. She managed to be assertive, but she was naturally a soft-spoken person who wasn't the center of the room. Still, with her unique brand of leadership, she made a tremendous impact on the lives of others through her highly relational style and mentored numerous people.

For many years, I struggled with feeling like a leader, even after I was assigned my first people management role at the age of twenty-three. It wasn't something that came to me naturally. Attending an "Introduction to Managing and Supervising Others" course was helpful for me, but some of the principles that I learned there didn't really make sense for me personally. Whenever

I tried some of the tactics from those trainings, it felt unnatural and didn't actually make me feel comfortable in my role as a leader. Like Neddy, I knew I needed to figure out how to make it work with who I was.

Ask yourself: What does leadership mean to you and what kind of leader do you want to be? Without getting into the semantics of how leadership differs from supervising or managing, I define leadership as the art of achieving a desired outcome through and with others. Most people learn to lead over time, and it is a skill that can be developed and practiced by anyone from any cultural background.

Just because someone is good at a skill doesn't necessarily mean they're going to be able to lead others effectively. How does being good at what you do translate into influencing others and motivating *them* to do good work? Those are different skills altogether. You might be the star striker on your soccer team, but does that mean you're the best person to coach the team as well? Even if you excel at performing some function, you might not have the skills (yet) to teach, coach, or help someone develop.

> **Leadership is the art of achieving a desired outcome through and with others.**

I get worried when I hear things like "This guy was born to lead," or "She's not really leadership material." These phrases assume a lot about who can be a leader, and I find that they're restrictive and untrue. This kind of thinking actually puts limitations on an individual's future career options because it assumes a fixed, rather than growth, mentality. Becoming a leader takes time, growth, and a deep understanding of how people operate. Anyone *can* become a good leader, but no one is automatically born with those skills; they must be developed and honed—and that starts with creating your own unique version of leadership.

Your life experiences and the skills you've already acquired will provide a solid foundation for your future leadership. If you haven't already, I encourage you to complete the Seven Stories exercise in appendix B. It will give you a great start at uncovering your *motivated skills* that you've used repeatedly throughout your life—these are skills that you're good at, that you enjoy doing, and that give you a sense of accomplishment.

What If You Don't Currently Manage People?

If you're currently in a role where you're not directly managing other people, all this can still apply to you. Try thinking about leadership in a broader way: you're probably managing multiple projects, working through various functions to get necessary information, or collaborating with vendors or external parties to influence their deliverables and get your work done. Think of it as your own "personal interaction model" while also recognizing that this work could be prepping you for a future leadership role if that is a genuine interest.

Creating Your Own Blueprint

What would a model look like that embodies the best version of yourself in a workplace context while allowing you to be your most authentic and productive self? If you define one that works for you (by showcasing your unique qualities and integrating attributes that are important to you) and you can feel good about putting it into action, then you'll be more likely to practice those behaviors! This doesn't mean you have to be rigid with it, either—the whole point is to think outside the box and adapt something that works for *you*.

To help you get there, I've put together a few preliminary activities designed to get you thinking about and visualizing your own model.

You'll start by asking a trusted friend or family member to answer a few questions about how they experience you. They have seen you in a variety of settings, so their responses can help illuminate what they perceive your values to be in light of the actions, behaviors, and tendencies they have observed over time.

Next, you will identify milestone moments or events that were pivotal or life-changing. When did those significant moments happen, and what role did you play?

Then, you'll think about what you've learned from your family. These lessons are your first "cultural values"—the beliefs, attitudes, and world-views that your family (and the generation before them) taught you, consciously or unconsciously. Because they're absorbed at a formative time in childhood, these values may be so automatic that you need to think deeply to identify them, and it may help to ask others for feedback. But understanding them can help you realize what values are ingrained in you and why. The process of naming these values will make you more conscious of them so you can do something with them. As part of this process, you'll complete a Venn diagram activity to help you think more critically about how your values have affected your behavior and how you might negotiate the differences between them.

After you complete all of these activities, you'll have the building blocks you need to craft your own model. Each building block represents an important step in designing your own leadership model. So, make sure you complete all three as best as you can.

Building Block 1: Learning How Your Family and Trusted Friends See You

 ## Interview a Close Friend or Family Member

Sit down with a close family member or a best friend and ask them the following questions:

- What are one or two key experiences that have shaped your understanding of me?

- What do you think my core values are?

    - What have I done in the past to show you that those are my values? What led you to make that observation?

    - What are some indicators of those values? What behaviors do I demonstrate that reflect those values?

Look over their answers and then ask yourself these questions:

- What was surprising to hear?

- Where do I think I absorbed those values?

- What did I learn about myself or the way that others view me that was new information?

Lastly, write down the phrases, words, or themes that jumped out at you during the interview:

_____

_____

_____

Building Block 2: Identifying the Experiences That Have Shaped You

Now, reflect on your life and think about the moments when what you were doing wasn't working anymore. Think of the times that left you feeling disoriented, when what you used to know or do was no longer effective. Think of a time when you stopped in your tracks and had to question how you responded or behaved in a particular situation. What did you have to shift, either dramatically or subtly? How did you behave differently afterward?

These moments usually happen (though not always) in a social context when you're interacting with people who are different from you in some way. For example, consider two girls who start playing on a boys' baseball team and realize the social dynamics are different from what they're used to. Do they keep playing the way they've been taught, or do they adapt to the new situation around them? Or imagine attending a fancy cocktail party for the first time in the United States. How would you figure out the rules of engagement, especially if you're coming from another country where these types of events are far from common? Or even imagine that you've failed a class in college and now you're being forced to acquire new study habits in order to pass the next time. Each of those life experiences, while initially uncomfortable, has the potential to teach the outsiders joining the group a new way of operating and communicating in a new culture.

 ## Key Learning Experiences

Brainstorm three key learning experiences that have thrust you into a new situation where you needed to adapt your way of thinking and acting. List them here. Feel free to use another piece of paper to write down others.

_____

_____

_____

_____

_____

Identifying Your Milestone Moments

After you identify your key learning experiences, fill in the blanks below to describe a specific situation that impacted you. Then, complete the following sentence to show what that experience taught you about yourself.

Key Learning Experience #1

The situation:

An important life lesson I learned from this was:

_____

_____

How does this affect how I do my work and my leadership or interaction style?

_____

_____

Key Learning Experience #2

The situation:

A key takeaway I learned about what I'm good at was:

_____

_____

How does this affect how I do my work and my leadership or interaction style?

_____

_____

Key Learning Experience #3

The situation:

My key understanding about what motivates people was:

_____

_____

How does this affect how I do my work and/or my leadership or interaction style?

_____

_____

Building Block 3: Bridging Your Cultural Values

 Personal Cultural Values vs. Workplace Cultural Values

In this activity, you'll compare, contrast, bridge, and reconcile your own cultural values with what is expected in your organization. This will give you a chance to think about how blending the two in a hybrid fashion can create a leadership model that you'll feel good about using.

1. **Name the values.**

   - In the oval on the left, list as many cultural values as you can that left an imprint on you from an early age. What did your parents, grandparents, and community teach you about the right way to behave and how to deal with authority figures? What behaviors were rewarded? Use a short, one-word descriptor to describe each of these values.

   - In the oval on the right, list the core principles or messages that are valued at your workplace. What does your company most value in its employees? What values repeatedly surface at your company?

Step 1: Naming the Values

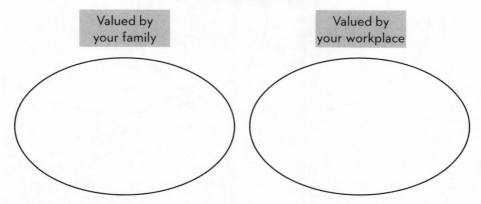

2. Evaluate or prioritize the values.

Underline the most important values inside the diagrams. Which ones are non-negotiables, both for yourself and your family as well as for your company?

3. Bridge the values.

As you step back and look at your diagram, how many core values overlap with each other? What could a combination of them look like?

Which ones need to be clarified and which values are at odds with each other?

In the Venn diagram, write the values that overlap in the middle part of the two circles. Keep the values that aren't overlapping in their respective circles.

Step 3: Bridging the Values

Valued by your family   Valued by your workplace

4. Make meaning of the values.

Now you'll reconcile the differences and identify any patterns that you see.

- *Compare:* What are the differences between the two diagrams? Which values were easy for you to identify and which ones were more difficult to unearth?

- *Contrast:* What's similar about the two sets of values? Which ones are at odds with each other?

- *Bridge:* Which of these could be integrated? Which combination will be most helpful to you to enable you to be an effective leader? What work needs to be done for this to happen? Which ones have you integrated already? What is something you're still working on? Which is most important to helping you achieve your career goals?

Now, let's take this one step further. Looking at the Venn diagram again, consider how your different values are contributing to your own traits as a leader.

For example, if "building relationships" was in the overlapping part of the circle, what does that look like from your cultural perspective? In your Asian community, how did your family members forge new relationships, and was it different from how your neighbors did it? How does that compare with how your coworkers relate to one another in your company? Then, think about what might happen when two very different perspectives come together. Here are a couple of examples:

- Humility and modesty + Boldly empowering teams = Quiet activator

- Group ownership of tasks + Getting buy-in = Effective implementer

Ask yourself:

- Can I be respectful of others and bold at the same time?

- Can I be quiet and still demonstrate a sense of confidence that others can recognize, even if I'm not the loudest person in the room?

- Can I be passionate about the business and still be empathetic about including my team members in decision-making?

While thinking through and reviewing where the two sets of values intersect, write out some areas of possibilities that may show up in your own leadership.

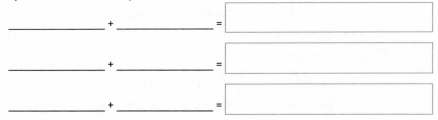

_____ + _____ = [   ]

_____ + _____ = [   ]

_____ + _____ = [   ]

Keep in mind that even with contrasting values, you can find a way to integrate your unique leadership. In my firm's leadership programs, I've often heard from Asian leaders something like "They expect us to be bold and crazy in our ideas in an effort to be innovative, but they don't see that we can be creative and generative without being a blowhard. Some of the people who've gotten ahead here have been overly political bullies who have alienated other people. I do it differently and I can drive tremendous results while leaving our team members' dignity intact!"

How does this actually show up? In your Venn diagram, it might break down to:

- **Family values:** Care for each other, nurture others, care for the team, be humble

- **Organization:** Win at all costs, beat the competition, drive results

- **Common ground:** We leverage our differences to win together. We operate with a highly competitive drive to win and get results, but we do it by working closely with each other to build high-trust relationships that break down silos and egos. We leverage our differences whenever possible to make the most of our diversity

Taking all of these core values and the possibilities within them, it's time to start identifying what you want to use in your own leadership. What conclusions can you draw from this exercise? How will this inform your leadership approach toward others? What needs to change in how you navigate your organizational culture? Up until now, you've probably been in a default mode when it comes to working with and managing others. Now, consider how you want to intentionally design your own leadership model to integrate all of these new perspectives.

Putting It All Together

 ## Create Your Own Visual Leadership Model

What are four or five core beliefs you'd like to embody as a leader? Which values are most important to you? How would you put your leadership approach together in a visual that represents the core elements?

Figure 6-1 shows an example of a leadership model of a Korean American executive in one of our leadership programs.

Example: Personal Leadership Model

FIGURE 6-1. How one Korean American executive defined his leadership model

Use the space below to draw your own model, sketch a picture, or write out something to depict the important aspects of how you want to work with others. Remember that you have the freedom to create something that makes sense for *you* and aligns with *your* core values. Let the sky be your limit!

Leveraging Your Quiet Strength to Elevate Others

David Moore, a production designer at Hallmark, is biracial (half Vietnamese, half white) and identifies as queer. Early in his childhood, his mother raised him to be as Western as possible. Consequently, he learned very little about his Vietnamese heritage. His journey has taken him from his birthplace in Vietnam to Europe to the tiny town of Knob Noster, Missouri, and into the US military and Desert Storm long before the policy of "Don't ask, don't tell." He later went to a faith-based college where he came out and was asked to leave.

He recalls being in a bad place in his young adult years: "It was that idea of shame, especially shaming my mother when I came out. She was fine with it, personally. She always said: 'You're still my son.' But she was also the matriarch of the Vietnamese [community] in our town, and there was this acute feeling that I had let them down—you don't bring shame on the community of Vietnamese people."

David has been at Hallmark for twenty-three years. "I'm at a place now where I actually like the idea of being different. It's a kind of a superpower, and what really sets me apart from somebody else. You know, I feel like it's because of my Asian-ness that [I] create the art that I create." He believes it's important not to make premature assumptions about people at the outset. David says, "Just because somebody comes from a particular place or looks a certain way does not mean that they're an expert on everything that you might associate with a person." For instance, it took a long time for him to think of himself as "leadership material," and his leadership potential wasn't always recognized by others at first. "I think it's because I'm very introverted. But now, I think if you ask people they would say, 'David's kind of a quiet one until you get to know him.'"

David embraced his leadership potential and his Asian identity through his work with the Asian American Resource Community at

Hallmark (AARCH) and through NAAAP, an association for Asian American professionals. He was a valued chair of AARCH for a year and serves in the Kansas City chapter of NAAAP.

When David was first tapped to lead AARCH, senior leaders had doubts about his candidacy because he was so quiet. They thought that he wasn't the "best choice." He proved them wrong.

What David has been able to open other people's eyes to is that fact that "Although I may be quiet, it doesn't mean I don't have good ideas. Look for the quiet people in your circle. There are a lot of great ideas percolating there, and I know many may not feel that they have the ability to share them, but it's there, you know? I hope this is the impact I'm having on people around me."

He expresses his leadership philosophy with conviction: "I want folks to know that I see them and desire to see their true authentic selves. Within the Namaste greeting is the action of bowing—I am also here to be of service to them. So, it's about acknowledging a person's existence, their humanity, their divinity, their skills, and contributions. And I want them to know I am here for them, to help them accomplish their goals/dreams, to clear a path if possible, to make connections if needed, to listen, to be present."

When David was ERG chair of AARCH at Hallmark, he ensured that they collaborated with every other ERG on an event that showed their intersections. "We received accolades and praise about the way we executed that event. And I realized then that my voice has an impact. That experience allowed me to dream that I could do just about anything. . . . I used to not see myself as leadership material because I don't 'look like that.' And I don't speak like that. *It's about building your own leadership style. I'm not being authentic if I become you. You can take bits and pieces from others and see what's been successful and what you admire about others, but how do you make it fit you?*"

Learn how to listen to the quiet people in your circle.

The Value of Crafting Your Leadership Model

I hope that delving into your life experiences and drafting your personal leadership model has taught you more about yourself and what you would like to share with the world.

At this point, you've named the key pivotal experiences that have shaped you as a leader. You've also identified specific learning from your cultural experience to inform how to bring yourself more fully to the workplace. The model represents your intention for the future, so it is right for it to be aspirational and to include practices that you are not yet demonstrating yet. It might seem like a reach for you at the outset. Ultimately, I want this to be a model for you to lean on when you're operating in the most integrated way.

Bringing Your Authentic Self to Work

When I asked Kim Cummings, senior vice president of HR at a children's hospital, how she lives out the challenge of "bringing her authentic self" to the workplace, she said, "Yes, I believe in that concept, but I also believe in phases. We have to be thoughtful not to say, 'This is me—take it or leave it!' as it takes a while for others to accept you or rather get to know you. I don't believe in the 'shock factor' just for the sake of it, either. For me, as a fun example, many people don't know that I have tattoos. Early on in my career I would hide them with Band-aids. There was a time when it was more of an exception than the rule to have a tattoo, and being in HR, I can tell you that it was definitely considered a taboo. Now I feel *absolutely comfortable* showing them. It actually gets people to ask questions about why I got *that* one, etc., and it starts a conversation that enables you to get to know others better."

Kim has found that the more appropriate you are in your confidence, the more of an impact you can have.

"So, when I bring my full self out there, whether it's on social media or other ways that we represent our organization, it has to make sense and have a degree of appropriateness. For example, I am a professional, mom, and friend; I have a deep sense of conviction about what's right and wrong to share in those roles. It's important for me to use my voice, and there will be people who don't react well to that . . . so I need to stand true to what I believe and work hard to demonstrate the behaviors that are consistent with those values."

Throughout our conversation, Kim's leadership voice and conviction came through loud and clear.

Remember that your model is not yet a perfectly finished product, and perhaps it never will be. There will be iteration involved. As with everything we have been working on together, it is important to start with something and try it out, then build from there. It's always beneficial to start with your own story, because that contains a unique and powerful experience. Once you have a leadership model you want to share with others, you're ready for the next stage of actionizing it. By leaning into it and using it, you can expand upon it as you try it out in the real world. Over time, you'll also spend less time and energy trying to hide (or do the corporate "dance") to figure out how to fit into your company.

Excelling in your leadership skills means putting into practice the behaviors and attitudes that you want to demonstrate to others. In the coming chapters, I will guide you through how you might do so by sharing your vision with the important stakeholders in your life and work.

Looking Forward: Leading with Cultural Fluency

*If you talk to a man in a language he understands,
that goes to his head. If you talk to him in his
language, that goes to his heart.*

—NELSON MANDELA

Throughout all of part II, we've looked at the practical ways in which you can start to create a new vision for your leadership. I've equipped you with tools for *how* to make your leadership your own, while helping to uncover your *why*.

But why does leading from an authentic place make such a difference? Research by van den Bosch and Taris shows that employees' perception of authentic leadership serves as the strongest predictor of job satisfaction and positively impacts work-related attitudes and happiness. Thus, it's crucial to show up with your most authentic self in order to become a culturally fluent leader.

Leading with authenticity comes from having a deeper understanding of your whole self. As someone who embodies the elements of more than one cultural perspective or identity, you bring an additive voice and a different point of view to your organization. Leading from a place of authenticity will tap into how you can use those multiple cultural perspectives—and will help you determine what's right for you for both in your life outside of work and inside your organization. Exploring that authenticity required examining your cultural experiences, your deeply held values, and the dynamic of insider/outsider experiences that have shaped you. All of this will (hopefully) make you stronger and better equipped to navigate the challenge of leadership in a rapidly changing workplace.

While leadership is about how you work with and impact others (your external world), if you want to do it right, you have to first look *inward* to learn what works about your approaches and what doesn't. Only once you tap into who you really are (both your superpowers as well as your imperfections) can you contribute fully in your organization and community. If you don't define *how* you will make that happen, you won't become better tomorrow than you are today. Working with other people and figuring out what makes them tick is often a mystery. People change. And change is guaranteed. Time and again, starting with a beginner's mindset and a willingness to declare who you want to be—while still being open to change—is key.

Excelling in your leadership skills means putting into practice the behaviors and attitudes that you want to demonstrate to others. Now that you have your first leadership model designed and ready to go, it's time to share your next steps with those who will directly inform and help further refine your plans. What do you *need from others* to begin putting your goals into action? What needs to change in how you navigate your organizational culture?

Next, in part III, I will guide you through how to share your vision with the important stakeholders in your life and provide you with more critical resources to support your leadership journey.

Key Learning Points

- You will be most effective when you're not conforming to preconceived ideas of what a leader looks and sounds like, but utilizing a style that is closely aligned to your core values.

- Perhaps the best thing about your future as a leader is that you will get to choose how you influence and work with others. You can think about it as a leadership model (or personal interaction model, if you're an individual contributor) that is custom-designed to help you succeed.

- Essential to this process is reflecting upon the key experiences in your life—pivotal moments, takeaways, and milestones—and choosing how you will best apply these learnings to the way you work and lead from this day forward.

- A crucial step in designing your leadership model is bridging the values learned in your family with those of your workplace. Where do these cultural values overlap or conflict?

- Creating a visual representation in the form of your personal leadership model can be enormously helpful for keeping you on track toward your development goals.

PART III

Thriving as a Culturally Fluent Leader

7

ENLARGING YOUR TENT

The Value of Networks and Community

*I alone cannot change the world, but I can cast
a stone across the waters to create many ripples.*

—MOTHER TERESA

When I was just starting out in my career, I believed that my main responsibility was to produce consistently good work and drive results for my firm's clients. As junior associates, we worked long hours—working through dinner at the office was the norm—so unless I was summoned to a meeting, it didn't occur to me to do anything other than "keep my head down" during the workday. I had a wakeup call one day when I noticed that a coworker frequently stopped by our manager's office when I thought she should have been diligently working at her desk. Imagine my confusion and shock when she said she was often just "shooting the breeze," and talking about sports, family, and her future career interests with our group head! I had known intuitively that networking was important, but it had never occurred to me that I could have anything but a business conversation with the head of our group. I realized that my coworker was creating a valuable relationship she might carry with her into the future, one that could yield connections and opportunities. Respecting someone in a position of authority was deeply embedded into my makeup, and I rarely reached out to superiors to engage in informal ways. No one ever taught me I had to create relationships outside the scope of my deliverables—and who had the time, anyway?

But the truth is that no one is an island, and this is especially true when it comes to how organizations function. We can't accomplish important work alone, and we don't become effective leaders alone, either. Whether you're trying to increase your influence or you're looking to advance in your company, connections are paramount to making that happen. Building a strong rapport with your manager is just one part of that. From the senior executive who puts your name in the ring for a highly visible leadership position to the peer in a different department who has your back—or someone outside the industry who offers moral support when your company is going through a downsizing—these relationships are valuable. Therefore, it's key to understand how to foster a community that will create the best possible conditions for putting your leadership skills into practice.

You've spent the previous part of the book getting a deeper understanding of yourself and articulating the kind of leader you want to become to go along with your main career objectives. Now we'll focus on creating the kind of meaningful connections that will help you become that effective leader you've envisioned. This will mean getting deeper in the relationships you have and growing your network by building community.

We'll start this work by grounding you in the components of a strong network, reflecting on the different types of networking experiences you've had, and then doing an activity to identify your current network base and what you ultimately want from it. We'll then focus on strengthening your network, which includes an analysis of why diversity is so critical to the community you develop around you.

If you find yourself at the cusp of the credibility building phase of your development as a leader, you'll want to pay special attention to the quality of those relationships. And building relationships requires time—both for investing in new ones and for cultivating the ones you already have. Why? Because organizations are more complex than ever. Matrix relationships that accompany cross-functional teams working across multiple time zones often have unclear ownership and reporting lines. As you respond to the divergent goals that different leaders set, it's not enough to be regarded as a strong contributor by your direct manager. And you can't depend on people in your functional unit to be the sole source of support. You must also build relationships that will help you move forward with your career goals *and* offer a sense of support and community when you need it.

Networking from an Authentic Place

If networking as a discipline conjures up images of schmoozing at cocktail parties or passing out business cards to anyone you meet, you're not alone: we've all seen the movies from the nineties where Wall Street men smarm their way through a workplace. True relationship building, however, is about getting to know people and showing them a piece of your authentic self as you offer help or ask for support, guidance, or the information you need to move forward. And it's okay to ask for guidance—as long as you do it appropriately. Showing an element of vulnerability helps connect people emotionally to your underlying need. Networking is just another venue to demonstrate the authentic "you."

In reality, networking is all about creating meaningful relationships that foster your personal *and* career growth. That includes forging true bonds with people who will challenge you and encourage you to step outside of your comfort zone. Sometimes, and with certain people, that may seem like a daunting (if not impossible) task, as this next leadership story demonstrates.

From Conflict to Mentorship: Making the Most of a Learning Experience with a Senior Leader

It wasn't the smoothest relationship right off the bat for Korean American Bryan MacDonald, the senior vice president of risk at BECU. Earlier in his career, a new executive had joined the organization and was spearheading an important initiative in a certain strategic direction. As he was rolling it out, Bryan recalls having a different opinion than this leader.

One day, at a meeting, their conflicting views came to light.

Bryan recalls: "When I voiced my opinion in a larger forum, I felt that there was a reaction from his side, and it wasn't positive. And [then] I thought [more about] that reaction: Was it on my part or his part? Reflecting on that, I took the time to think through what he was facing as a new leader, what challenges might be in front of him, and how his reaction could have been from me publicly springing a dissonant view [on him]." Bryan went to the leader after the meeting to apologize for how he presented his view. "I had to balance what I felt was the right way to do it relative to what his position was in authority—but more than that, what he needed as a leader."

It turns out, this executive valued team alignment in such meetings and discussion of differing views beforehand. Along the way, Bryan recognized that his own ability to visualize processes and concepts was effective in connecting with the leader. Moving forward, whenever they discussed intricate operational issues or challenges, Bryan would go to the whiteboard to jot down the process as he explained it, giving the leader a chance to confirm or challenge assumptions along the way. This ensured that everything was crystal clear and that Bryan's mentor could visualize what Bryan was doing and thinking. He appreciated that Bryan worked at flexing his style to connect with him in a helpful way.

Today, the executive is a close friend of Bryan's. As he thinks about that experience, Bryan counts it as a valuable learning opportunity that ended up yielding positive fruit. "That could have gone a lot of different ways, but I feel like recognizing the situation from his perspective allowed me to consider things from an alternative point of view, right? But more than that, to understand the pressures, the feelings, all that was going on, from a leader's perspective. Through that shared experience, we established a deep trust that still stands today." By taking both of their perspectives into account, Bryan was able to convey his ideas more clearly *and* create a meaningful relationship that remains constructive to this day. He created a genuine connection by listening, being open to adapting to, and applying what this particular relationship needed.

The Value of Expanding Your Community

Today, I urge people to embrace networking as a parallel career path. And while you might cower at Keith Ferrazzi's suggestion in *Never Eat Alone* to speak to fifty people a day to build your network, you can appreciate its underlying philosophy: if you concentrate on building your network, the stronger and better it will get. Most of us couldn't come close to speaking to so many people in one day! However, there is great value in regular, intentional outreach to meet people outside of your immediate circle, even strangers.

Absolutely no one has the corner of the market on relationships. Even if you tend toward introversion, you never know where your path will lead or what kinds of people you might meet—so be open to them. In the United States, a person will hold an average of twelve jobs in their lifetime, so your current job will not necessarily be your last. In addition to jobs, you'll likely have additional interests, such as volunteer work, sports and hobbies, and activities at your place of worship or your kids' schools. All of your contacts are valuable, and you never know who will be a resource for you (or you for them).

How long has it been since you took a long, hard look at your business and social networks? Are you engaging with people whose areas of interest are symbiotic with yours? Are you doing things you find interesting with people you admire or enjoying spending time with? If the answer is no, then it might be time to make networking a priority in your life.

Aligning with the Rhythms of Your Life

The way you choose to nurture your networks has to make sense for you. For example, we all have circadian rhythms. My neighbor, a self-professed night owl, decided as a New Year's resolution to try working out in the gym before sunrise in an effort to get it in before the baby woke up and the emails started streaming in. It did not last. His energy level in the morning was low, and he wasn't able to exert the kind of vigor he did in the evening. He went back to working out after dinner, which was the optimal time for him.

It's hard to do something that's completely outside of the realm of what we find comfortable, and that applies to networking as well. Think about how you can weave connecting with people naturally into your life. I once attended an event where I was the only person of Asian descent and the only woman under the age of fifty. After getting over my initial discomfort and feeling completely out of place, I ended up meeting a colleague who has helped me think about my business differently over the years, and I've been able to provide support to his work as well. Going to large events can open you up to people you've never met, but the work of building those new relationships always requires following up one-on-one. You can always do a mix of both, based on your preferences. The point is that in order to make building relationships a part of your natural activities, it has to follow the rhythm of how you prefer to work and play. You might enjoy going out and meeting new people, or maybe the idea of going to a business networking event or a conference is draining. If you detest parties or large events, seek out functions where you can go with a buddy and be introduced to specific people by getting to know the host ahead of time. You can also ask people you know already to introduce you to new people. One way to do that is to get specific: "One goal I have in the new year is to speak to people who are using AI in ways that positively affect society. If you know anyone who fits that description, I'd really appreciate an introduction, and I'll be sure to return the favor one day."

Playing the Long Game in Networking

The currency of real networking is not greed but generosity.

—KEITH FERRAZZI, *Never Eat Alone*

The best way to network is to:

- Be intentional and invest time into widening your tent by building new relationships outside of your circle.

- Start with people you get a good feeling from. While this isn't sufficient for a strong long-term relationship, it is often necessary, especially at the outset.

- Create a mutually beneficial relationship. This doesn't have to happen at once, but the intent of networking is to help each other, so always offer to return the favor, even if you're not able to do so immediately.

- Aim to build trust and goodwill over a period of time. Everyone can spot the person who's in it just for connections. Work on building true relationships and follow up on your connections, recognizing that trust takes time.

Successful networking is about seeking ways to meet new people and showing your interest and willingness to interact and support them. Simply asking trusted colleagues, friends, and even your family for referrals to people you'd like to get to know is a good way to start. Then follow through on the important ones and stay in touch with them.

Professional organizations related to your area of expertise or your goals are another place to grow your network. If you join a professional organization, you can volunteer for a committee, help plan or host an event at your company for their members, or volunteer to raise funds. I've *never* met a professional association that has said no to someone who wants to call potential donors!

There are many ways to create ties with new people or strengthen the ones you currently have. The key to building new relationships is to work within the scope of who you are and *what you enjoy*, not to turn it into a task that's overwhelming for you.

The High Cost of Not Having Close Relationships

Loneliness kills. It's as powerful as smoking or alcoholism.

—ROBERT WALDINGER, Harvard Study of Adult Development

Apart from helping you develop your career and get things done more efficiently, having strong relationships has health benefits too.

One study, which looked at data from over 309,000 people, showed that not having strong relationships increased the risk of premature death from all causes by 50 percent, which has an effect on your mortality comparable to smoking fifteen cigarettes a day and a greater effect than physical inactivity or obesity. When you demonstrate caring behaviors, you trigger the release of stress-reducing hormones. The relationships in your life don't have to be good all the time, but they are essential for longevity and well-being.

Embracing the Counterintuitive Power of Weak Ties

A friend may be waiting behind a stranger's face.

—MAYA ANGELOU, Letter to My Daughter

Contrary to popular belief, research shows that it's *not* the people who are closest to us (i.e., family and close friends) who are more likely to find us jobs or secure us new contracts. In fact, it's typically *their* friends and contacts who are more likely to help us the most.

I recently interviewed Dr. Naava Frank, who specializes in communities of practice in nonprofits and the value of networks, to discuss the importance of learning socially with other people. She told me, "There are two different types of relationships: bonding and bridging. When you connect with people who are similar and close to you, that's bonding. They share interests; [they] could live on the same block or be your BFF at your gym. And bonding yields affinity, team efficiency, depth, support, and community. The other kind of people you want to connect to leads to bridging. This type of connecting reaches across a variety of differences to people who you might not feel as comfortable with. These bridging relationships lead to new access, resources, and new ways of thinking and doing things."

As you grow in your leadership, you need to build *both* kinds of connections, because they yield different results. Ask yourself: Am I going for depth or innovation? What kind of relationship could foster that, one that bonds or one that bridges? The process of bonding (with your intramural baseball team, your neighbors, etc.) may be easier, but bridging across differences (the weak ties) is where unexpected innovation can spark. Ultimately, a bridging connection is more likely to lead to a new job or a new opportunity.

That said, you shouldn't neglect to ask those close to you to make introductions to people who could help you reach your goals. I generally don't post about my work accomplishments on my personal social networks, tending to share my work updates, articles, and speaking engagements on LinkedIn instead. But one year, when I published an article that I was especially proud of, I put it on Facebook to share with my friends and family. The response I got from that one post was beyond what I could have hoped for; most people didn't know exactly what I do for a living, and they were excited to read what I had written. Moreover, they found the advice helpful. This led to my friends signing up to receive my newsletter, and later that year, I received three referrals who became clients I still have to this day. It was the mix of both weak and strong ties that yielded positive benefits. We'll take a look at both as you examine your current network.

Connecting to the Power of Your Network

How might networking affect your leadership trajectory and accelerate your career development? Let's start by identifying the reach and power of the relationships you already have and how they have benefited you.

Connecting the Past and the Present

1. How has networking helped you in the past? Highlight one or two moments in your life where networking has played a key role in your career.

One leader's example: *Once, I had a hard time recovering from an error that I had made on a project. After it happened, my mentor took me to dinner and gave me the most encouraging pep talk of my life. My confidence was restored because he made me feel like I had worth and that my identity wasn't tied up with my work output. He knew that my failure was hard for me to recover from. It helped me to be less critical of myself.*

2. Now let's identify key connections in your current network. Using the Critical Stakeholders Clustergram, put yourself in the middle and write in the names of the individuals who are the main critical stakeholders in your professional life in the different spokes (i.e., your most important contacts).

3. Before we proceed to expanding your network, let's analyze your current one. Label each connection in the clustergram as Exceptional, Good, or Needs Improvement. Next to their names, add the number of years you've been connected to them.

Critical Stakeholders Clustergram

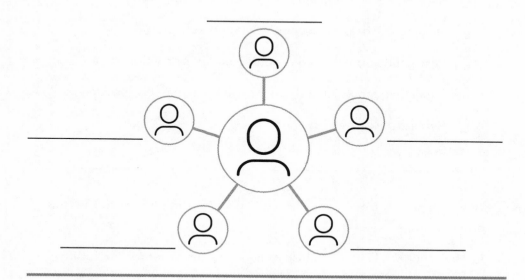

 # Expanding Your Network: Building New Relationships

What are your primary reasons for building your network at this time? Check off as many as you wish.

- ☐ Personal enrichment

- ☐ Keeping up with others in my current or future industry or field

- ☐ Finding a new job

- ☐ Seeking potential mentors

- ☐ Learning from others

- ☐ Increasing my influence in the organization

☐ Expanding my own visibility

☐ Seeking board opportunities (nonprofit or corporate)

☐ Helping my local community/volunteering

☐ Post-pandemic expansion—getting out of my comfort zone

☐ Expanding cross-cultural or cross-generational relationships

☐ Other (specify below)

_____

Now, look over the items you checked off and put a star next to your top priorities.

1. How could building relationships help you get closer to your future personal and professional goals?

_____

2. What new relationships would you like to build? Brainstorm a list here, populating it with names or roles.

1. _____

2. _____

3. _____

4. _____

5. _____

Strengthening Your Network

Now, let's identify the types of relationships you already have and how you might go about strengthening those valuable connections (or building new ones).

Assessing Your Network for Future Development

Taking stock: Let's assess your network and what might be missing. Where should you invest more time in the coming year? Staying in an echo chamber won't be helpful when it comes to making effective business decisions.

Take a closer look at the Critical Stakeholders Clustergram you just completed. How diverse is your network? Who are you getting new information from? Where are you getting answers to difficult problems? Who's missing?

Give yourself a rating on these elements (on a scale from 1 = nonexistent to 5 = deep and wide network of relationships):

Overall diversity of your network	1	2	3	4	5
People from other cultural/ethnic/racial backgrounds	1	2	3	4	5
People from other departments/functions/regions	1	2	3	4	5
People from other industries	1	2	3	4	5
People who are one or two levels above you	1	2	3	4	5
People who are one or two levels below you	1	2	3	4	5
Potential mentors	1	2	3	4	5
Potential proteges	1	2	3	4	5

If you chose 4 or 5 for most of these, then you already have a pretty diverse network. If you circled more 1s or 2s, there might be some gaps in your network. This could point you to alternative connections you might like to foster.

Bonding: Focusing on Specific Relationships

Now think of a few relationships that you'd like to strengthen. List a few ways that this relationship might be a source of support for you, and also how you could be a resource to them.

NAME	CURRENT RELATIONSHIP TO YOU	HOW THEY MIGHT HELP	HOW YOU MIGHT HELP	N (NEW) OR E (EXISTING)
Example: John Doe	Former manager who went to a new company	Introduce you to his contacts	Support his efforts to appoint new volunteers to his nonprofit	Existing

Bridging: Getting Out and Connecting

With new relationships, it's particularly important to show interest in what people do and what they're passionate about. Maintaining those relationships involves doing the little things to keep that connection alive, such as affirming their accomplishments and changes to their work. Seeing that you value your relationships can make a big imprint on the people you're connecting with.

Which of these activities resonate with you?

- [ ] Maintain contact by email

- [ ] Send them a relevant article that they may find helpful

- [ ] Provide an update on your current project and ask for specific advice

- [ ] Invite them to a fundraising event at your nonprofit

- [ ] Share an accomplishment of yours at work

- [ ] Offer to support their favorite charity

- [ ] Attend a sporting event together

- [ ] Support them on LinkedIn or social media when they change jobs, post an accomplishment, get promoted, and the like

- [ ] Take them to lunch on their birthday

- [ ] Take a virtual coffee break with them

When my daughter was born, a business contact gifted us with a Boston Bruins baseball hat. While it wasn't the fanciest or most expensive gift, it was the most memorable one, as it showed that this individual took the time to remember that we had an emotional connection to hockey and the Bruins. We've never forgotten it, and it's become my go-to memory when I'm considering how to reach out to people and show them that I'm interested in a meaningful connection. Consider how you can show people you care in a similarly thoughtful way that makes it clear you're paying attention.

How Diverse Is Your Network?

If everyone in your professional network is similar to you—all from the same background, same cultural perspective, same age demographic, and with similar work experiences—there's a limit (for both you and for them) to the new ideas or growth you'll experience. Having the same outlook on the world can be comforting, but it's not pushing you to think differently or to consider other perspectives. It maintains a limited worldview in a connected society that's constantly changing. A huge barrier to innovation is the day-to-day rituals that keep us from seeing things through a new lens. Staying in one small corner of the world won't help you make connections that might lead to emerging customer segments.

If your network isn't as diverse as you'd like it to be, consider what social networks you're a part of. Maybe this means getting more involved in your local neighborhood or joining an organization where you'll meet people who share a hobby but come from different walks of life. Maybe this means connecting more deeply with others on your work team who come from a different cultural background. If networking within your company, I recommend considering influential people (regardless of level) who have an array of broad interests. People who are two or three levels above you in an organizational hierarchy are also great contacts to have. One overlooked reason for networking is that it allows you to collect external, alternative perspectives from a variety of important sources so that you can make wiser, more informed decisions about something you care about in your life. This is also why having a diverse network can be incredibly helpful; the more you are exposed to other perspectives, the more you'll be able to understand differing points of view.

Now that you understand the value of having a diverse and broad network, let's look at your personal objectives.

Enlisting Support from Managers and Higher-Ups

Building your network and enlisting support from managers and higher-ups is a strategic and lifelong process that can help you navigate major shifts in your career as you grow to the "expert" level. This process should be consistent, genuine, and mutual. Filipino American Angela* recalls a time when she knew she needed more support from the leaders at her managers' level. "About two years before a significant promotion, I needed a manager who would advocate for me, who would speak about my credentials in the 'handling' conversations in evaluation committees." She knew that not doing so in prior years had hurt her visibility. Angela reached out to various leaders throughout the year to get on their radar about her current projects and the great wins she was seeing. Not only did this boost her visibility, but it also had the benefit of allowing Angela to strengthen her understanding of the leaders' challenges. Three years later, she got a job working in one of the senior vice president's business units simply from taking that initiative and growing her connections. This approach of reaching out and making her contributions known helped her create a genuine relationship that later led to her promotion.

Perhaps you have some trepidation about reaching "up" to manage the power gap and build relationships with your superiors, but understand that it may be expected of you. The key is to be prepared, as much as possible, for whatever might come back at you when you do reach out. It's important for your managers to meet you where you are, but you can make the effort as well. Here are a few tips for getting started:

- Prepare to respond to a few introductory questions to imagine where the conversation will go.

- Prepare a pitch for what you'd like to discuss and how you want them to help.

---

* Pseudonyms throughout the book are indicated by an asterisk.

- Approach the leader with a specific ask, ideally one that leverages their unique knowledge.

Here are a few specific suggestions to get the conversation started:

> I have updated my development plan and I would like to discuss it with you. I'd love your take on any other resources you might recommend for me.

> Your growth strategy with _____ is going to make a huge impact, and I'm interested in getting more practice/experience/skills in that area. Your feedback would be really helpful and timely.

> I just finished this fantastic leadership program! As part of that, I've been building my own vision for how I want to engage my team as we go through this aggressive growth period. I've come up with a model to try out; your input would be helpful. There are a few directions I'm batting around that I'd like to run by you.

You already know it's important to enlist the support of your managers, but what if you work for someone who isn't supportive? While many of us will have managers who are eager to help us excel, unfortunately, some of us will not. If you work for an employer who doesn't seem to care about how you bring your full self to work, then consider these three options:

- Become a change agent at your organization. Some people believe that you need to have a certain title to drive change or create a different culture, but you can do this at any level. Your voice matters.

- Start looking for fields or industries that might be a more conducive environment for your gifts and talents. I'm *not* saying you should quit your job before you have a plan, but if your organization simply isn't open to change or growth, this might be your only option.

- Identify what you can do to work and learn as best as you can while you're in your current role. Use this experience to build relationships internally with people. Ultimately, you want to work for the right person, but if that's not currently possible, then think about how you can still use your position to network and create fruitful relationships with your peers that will make it more pleasant for you in the meantime.

You can't always control who you work for, but you can ask about the reputation of the organization's leaders before you take a new role. This can also help you understand how to navigate the culture of the organization you're about to enter. And I can say from personal experience: no one bonds as much as coworkers with an unsupportive boss!

The Importance of Mentors, Allies, and Peers

When David Nguyen, a director in the Digital Marketing Team at Putnam Investments, was first starting out in his career, he received advice from a friend, a senior female executive. She was very petite in stature (under five feet tall), but she had a commanding executive presence. "When I asked her what it's like being the only Asian in a boardroom full of men, she said, 'I don't focus on the fact that I'm the Asian minority in the room. I think to myself: I deserve to be in the room just as much as these white men; I founded the company years ago and I'm part of the leadership team.'"

David never forgot her words, and the underlying mentality that she modeled was something that has been instilled in his psyche ever since. "Now I aim to enter every situation with the mindset of 'I totally deserve to be here!'" He found a mentor and ally in this senior leader, who helped him understand what it meant to be Asian in his organization and who ended up becoming someone he could turn to for advice. And while she wasn't a direct peer, she did provide him with a safe space and essential wisdom that helped him find his place within his leadership.

This kind of allyship is essential to creating strong ties with those around you, and your peers with whom you've built a positive reputation are a great place to start amassing allies. If you get to know your peers on a personal level and listen for the ways you might be able to assist them, then you'll be creating a genuine relationship that could turn into help and support for you as well. Again, most people can sense inauthenticity immediately, especially when it comes to networking, so it's important to do this from a place of genuine connection rather than trying to use people to get ahead.

But there are deeper, more powerful reasons to connect with your peers. In times of trouble, your coworkers from a different demographic or ethnic group will greatly appreciate an ally. If something has happened in the news (like the civil unrest after George Floyd's murder or the anti-Asian violence in recent years), people might be hurting, scared, angry, or feeling one of a dozen other emotions. They might even be fearful of going outside, let alone going to the office. Gently ask what you can do to show your support. *A sincere and simple approach to show that you care is best here*:

> "Jenny, I won't pretend to know what you're thinking or feeling, but I want you to know I'm very concerned about what's going on in our neighborhood. If I can do anything, I want to be a resource for you. Or if you just want to talk about it, I'm here for that too."

> "Minh, how can I help? If you're feeling unsafe in any way, I want to help."

In general, developing allies under any circumstances requires careful listening, clear communication, commitment, and follow-through. Allies can be developed strategically to fulfill many purposes. Consider these scenarios:

- A white male ally who can empathize with the pain of being discriminated against calls out an insensitive comment that he overhears in casual conversation.

- A young lawyer develops allies to help her navigate politics when it comes to getting selected for critical client projects that position her for partnership.

- A soccer parent develops a network of allies to make sure the kids have safe transportation to and from practices and games.

What group of people best represents you—or the *future* you? What kind of ally do you want to be for the people around you? Networking and creating new relationships isn't just for enrichment and career support; it also creates solidarity and a sense of unity when communities are hurting.

Creating Community through Allies to Drive Innovation

We had to disrupt how the company viewed DEI and its ERGs.
—MICHAEL GONZALES

When Michael Gonzales was tapped to be the new chief diversity officer at Hallmark, he asked the CEO for the kind of support he would need if he were to take on that position. Michael was clear that he didn't want the diversity, equity, and inclusion (DEI) office utilized only to provide support to the ERGs around "celebrations" of ethnic holidays or Women's History Month.

"I wanted to broaden the impact of DEI at Hallmark," says Michael. He knew the potential it would have on the business. At first, Don, the CEO, was somewhat hesitant. "He said, 'Go and explore but don't do something so drastic or suggest something that's so out there that it's risky to our vision and branding.'"

Michael advocated for the Hallmark Asian network and worked with his colleagues to launch new product lines for the organization. "We had to disrupt the everyday mindset," he recalls. He worked with multiple ERGs that reported to him to achieve these goals. The Asian ERG and the LGBT ERG were the first two to succeed in helping colleagues from Creative and Marketing understand the value (and revenue potential) of creating cards and products specific to their communities. But first, they had to show the critical decision makers the return on investment (ROI) potential of the multicultural consumer base outside its corporate walls.

"We knew we had to be a positive disruption when presenting our business cases. So each ERG told a story about their community, celebrations, shopping patterns, family/community values, etc., closing with data that showed the buying power, populations, buying habits, and dollar spends.

The cases that we made were compelling and impossible to ignore. The Asian American demographic in the US represented $780 billion in market share and was the fastest-growing middle class. Out of that initiative, three new card lines were launched."

But Michael's team didn't stop there. "Once we got the Asian cards created, we connected with the Asian ERG at Walgreens and said, 'Hey, there's something here for you to look at.' We had already established ties with them as a retail partner who was already carrying our new LGBT line." By combining their resources, the ERGs were able to make a major change within the company.

Allies have the power to forge strong ties between our communities. By helping each other, both the LGBT ERG and the Asian ERG at Hallmark contributed value-added, lasting changes that continue to impact the bottom line.

Valuing Your Employee Resource Groups

Employee resource groups can provide a meaningful community within an organization that helps employees feel valued. Ivan Lee, director of Diversity, Equity and Inclusion at Elastic, noted, "ERGs are relatively new here (formalized in 2021), but [Elastic has] leapfrogged initiatives at peer companies by providing a budget for every ERG as well as industry-leading compensation for ERG leaders. Only a handful of companies pay their ERG leads (LinkedIn is the most well-known) and it speaks volumes to how we ensure that value-add labor associated with ERG leadership positions (which have a direct impact on business outcomes) are compensated."

The Power of Community in Times of Crisis

The fear was real.

I remember the first time I took the subway after Michelle Go was pushed off the platform at the Times Square R train station. On the news, I had watched the rise in disturbing incidents against the Asian community, including our elders being spit on or attacked, both verbally and physically. We were hypervigilant about our physical surroundings, especially on public transportation. That day, I got a seat in the subway car and noticed an Asian guy sitting across from me. We made eye contact and it was definitely a look of, *I've got your back if anything happens here*. It was a visceral reaction, but somehow I felt a sense of connection with this stranger, who I knew felt the same concern about the state of the world and his safety.

When I started to see executive leaders having listening sessions with Asian employees to understand their experience, I saw that these fears were not isolated. In those sessions, no one felt like they were the only one who had experienced a microaggression or insensitive comment in their school or workplace. Thankfully, the recent events gave rise to new advocacy organizations and new muscle to others. For the Asian American community, where many were not used to using their voices to speak out against bias incidents, these resources helped to create a sense of solidarity that they were not alone and helped them gain strength from the power of community.

Providing Strength in a Time of Crisis: Stop AAPI Hate

On March 19, 2020, at the height of anti-Asian discrimination, when incidents were happening daily, the online reporting portal Stop AAPI Hate was launched as the go-to resource for the Asian American community. In the days that followed, thousands of reports of verbal harassment and physical assault were logged. By the end of 2021, over ten thousand incidents had been reported. Stop AAPI Hate was founded by Russell Jeung, Cynthia Choi, and Manjusha Kulkarni, who recognized the need to document the rise of COVID-19-related anti-Asian racism in the early stages of the global pandemic. While many in the Asian American community had experienced these incidents firsthand, the attacks were often unreported by media and overlooked by others. The site was intended to make it easier for Asian Americans to report incidents of racism they experienced, ranging from physical violence to name calling in schools.

While Asian Americans were encouraged to report an incident to the police, Stop AAPI Hate became a helpful repository to log the numerous incidents that had happened. When a driver called out a racial slur as my son was crossing the street, we immediately reported this incident on the Stop AAPI Hate site and found comfort in making our community aware of what had happened.

In November 2023, Stop AAPI Hate announced two new advancements designed to deepen collective understanding of anti-AAPI racism and discrimination: a data visualization tool and an updated system for processing reported hate acts, which now includes the new categories of "institutional hate" and "societal hate." Stop AAPI Hate has become a valuable resource for amplifying Asian American voices.

The more you advance in your leadership, the more you'll find yourself in a position to help your larger community. These connections are critical lifelines for us, both for our development as leaders and as a way to personally give us a voice in our community. They are truly investments in our future. And as we've been discussing, relationships are not built overnight anyway!

But relationships do begin with intentional network building and the power of reaching out to those around you for help, support, and solidarity.

We cannot do it alone, and creating lasting relationships can not only help you advance your career but can help give your life more meaning and purpose.

NOTE See appendix A for a list of organizations that you might want to volunteer with.

Key Learning Points

- The value of your networks (personal and professional) and community can't be underestimated. It's critical to foster authentic connections with those who can help you make your future leadership vision a reality. An equally important part of this process is paying it forward by offering your support to others.

- In addition to aiding career development, networks can provide crucial support in other circumstances, such as when you're trying to enact change in an organization or navigating a difficult conflict.

- Identify the network you have been developing and look for ways to strengthen it. How diverse is it? And how diverse *could* it be? Does it align with your goals?

- Consider new relationships that would be beneficial. Start with tangible leads such as employee resource groups in your organization as well as less obvious ones that might be right in your community.

8

NETWORKING AND MANAGING YOUR PRESENCE IN THE DIGITAL AGE

*Technology, like art, is a soaring
exercise of the human imagination.*

—DANIEL BELL, *The Winding Passage: Essays
and Sociological Journeys, 1960–1980*

No matter how you feel about Zoom, Teams, Skype, and other virtual meeting platforms, the digital environment is here to stay.

During an early Zoom meeting with a client at the start of the pandemic, I used a huge physical pop-up backdrop since all the nice green screens were sold out due to the lockdown. Right in the middle of the call, the screen disengaged and fell on top of my head—thankfully, everyone had a sense of humor about it! Looking back on it now, I'm reminded how far we've come. Even though inexplicable glitches arise, most can be fixed quickly, like when your headset doesn't connect to Zoom on a particular day or your mic isn't working. . . ah, but then it does work, and it feels like a miracle! What was once foreign to me and an inconvenience at best has become my go-to form of communicating with others.

Today, most of us see the value of a digital environment, and even our grandparents are fluent in the use of virtual meeting platforms. There's a lot to be said in favor of connecting digitally. It allows us to work remotely when we need to and cuts down on commuting time, and it's helpful to see people's faces in the absence of an in-person environment. Then again, there are other challenges to navigate—and one of those is learning how to create genuine connections across that screen.

Recognizing and Responding to Biases in the Hybrid Environment

One thing we've learned from virtual meetings is that there are biases even in those settings! Communication research has shown that face-to-face, in-person interaction is the best way to conduct business and develop relationships. This allows most people to pick up on not just the words that you're trying to convey, but the tone, body language, eye contact, and gestures. For people who have high-context communication styles, the context and in-person experience provides critical information.

Many Asian Americans have reported to me that they struggled to build relationships over Zoom during the pandemic. Furthermore, the increasing reliance on digital environments exacerbates the insider/outsider dynamic. I worked with one company with a strong in-person culture that values one-on-one interpersonal exchanges to build camaraderie. In this company, if you're not working on meaningful projects, then you are disposable. Unfortunately, newer workers, as well as those from diverse cultural backgrounds, found it hard to develop relationships with senior leaders. Because many of their colleagues had already established go-to people whom they had known prior to the pandemic, they didn't need to offer the work to coworkers who were "untested."

Gaining Visibility and Navigating the Digital Space

There you are onscreen. When the virtual meeting starts, you're one face in a group of boxes, and no box is bigger than another. There's no real pre-meeting small talk or banter, unless it's a group that's been working together for a long time. You can't cross the room to introduce yourself to someone privately, and it's hard to read the nonverbal messages that are so important when it comes to human interaction. How do you interpret someone having his video camera turned off? Does he not want to be there? Or did he have an emergency to take care of? Another colleague is staring at something offscreen. Is she uncomfortable or just distracted? These are just a few of the issues you face in a digital environment.

Scholars Richard Daft and Robert Lengel defined the *media richness theory* as a way to evaluate the richness of communication media types, such as videoconferencing and email. The more complex your work task, the more difficult it can be to communicate across certain platforms. A text or email cannot reproduce voice tone and visual cues like body language, so it's less "rich" than videoconferencing, which transmits gestures and body language along with verbal communication. Of course, the richest of all communication approaches is a face-to-face encounter. As fortunate as it was that we were able to continue doing business during the global pandemic, the digital environment has posed challenges for different personality types, as well as for those who are used to operating in different cultural contexts.

It's trickier to understand the meaning behind eye contact (or lack thereof), physical movements, and body language on a virtual platform. You might have been raised with social norms that were considered "correct" by your parents or in their countries of origin that differ from those of your colleagues. Furthermore, your colleagues in different parts of the world might come from high-context cultures—where values and social norms are often shown through a person's mannerisms or tone, and silence can have different meanings. This is true of many Asian cultural spaces, which have expressions like *kuuki yomeru* ("reading the air"), a Japanese term for reading between the lines, and *noonchi* ("eye power"), a Korean word referring to the art of gauging others' moods in a particular situation. When I was a teenager, my mom often would tell me, "You don't have noonchi" in certain social situations. In cultures where so much meaning is conveyed by nuance and nonverbals and picking up on the subtle shifts in others' body language and mood, it can be particularly difficult to communicate over platforms that allow you less access to these bodily cues.

This is why paying particular attention to cultural differences is crucial when communicating—both in digital spaces *and* face to face. Not all cultures communicate out loud, but for Americans and other cultural groups who are used to direct communication, this can be difficult to understand. Heck, it's even difficult for those of us or our children who didn't grow up in Asia and need to learn this type of nonverbal communication before seeing grandparents or when visiting extended family in Asia. It's not always easy to realize that other people communicate in different ways than you. But in the digital space, it's even more important to be aware of how differences in communication styles can affect how people are reacting and engaging.

It's imperative that we give each other grace while still trying to understand that in every encounter, messages and perceptions are being subtly transmitted (see figure 8-1). Ask yourself: Is my audience more emotionally expressive than I am? Or less? Remember, changes in tone of voice, eye movements, and seemingly vague answers to direct questions are all hints that you may need to better understand and then interpret what someone is telling you. Even over a screen, you can start to gauge these nuances in behavior—and throughout this chapter, I'll give you some concrete tips for doing so.

Communication

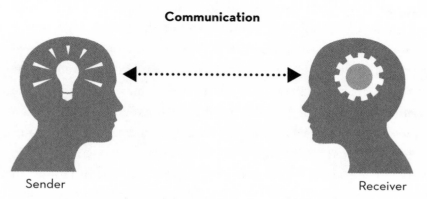

Sender   Receiver

FIGURE 8-1. Communicating across styles

Considering Your Audience

Keeping a relaxed, pleasant, and neutral expression is a good way to start when you don't have a lot of information about your audience. Depending on who you're addressing, you may need to get accustomed to their preferences. If you have an easy smile, that can sometimes be misinterpreted as approval. If you're more reserved and you're working with an audience that's largely used to a more expressive style, there's a risk of being seen as detached or uninterested.

Henry,* a white American leader who has a very animated, expressive style, was not initially seen as a credible leader when he presented to senior management in the regional offices in Asia, and he didn't immediately garner respect from his local team members either. If you're emotionally expressive in a dominant culture space that's more reserved in its communication style, there's a risk that you may be considered "too much" or "over the top." Either way, it's important to understand the intention and meaning behind your approach and to seek to create some shared meaning if there is potential for miscommunication. But that could just be a culture's natural state of being—or their cultural comfort zone.

If you tend to be emotionally reserved in your speech and facial expressions, keep an eye on how others engage with you over the screen. Come to a meeting knowing that you might have to stretch beyond your comfort zone and verbalize how you're feeling to demonstrate support for something. This might mean actually saying, "I'm thrilled about working on this new initiative with you; you can count on my support when it's time to implement it for our business." Particularly if you're working with people who are used to seeing more enthusiasm, saying, "I'm excited to hear that we're about to kick off this long-awaited project!" will help convey your enthusiasm.

Try to pay attention to how others are doing in a meeting even as you're working to make your own connections. If you're not sure how to read the dynamics of a meeting on an emotional level, then reach out to others for feedback shortly after to understand what might have transpired from another point of view. This is absolutely essential to do if you are operating across regions, as there are likely to be intercultural tensions stewing under the surface.

Managing Your Presence Virtually

Networking via the internet should be rooted in the same principles as traditional face-to-face, old-school networking: you're identifying the mutual benefits of connecting with each other and you're building that relationship over time. Manners still count when you send an email or a text with networking contacts. When following up after a meeting in an email, be brief and get to the point in one or two sentences; people's attention spans might be shorter in an online environment. Many executives have confessed to me that they receive up to two hundred emails every day, so they don't have time for lengthy correspondence. But there are a lot of ways to network over the internet; from LinkedIn to X (formerly Twitter), people are creating connections in digital spaces through shared interests or because they work in similar fields. If you work in a creative industry, perhaps you're even connecting over other social media—reacting to stories on Instagram or reposting photos on Facebook. These casual encounters can have a lasting effect; the more visible you are in someone's life and support what they're doing, the more they tend to think about you as a valuable connection.

Building a relationship via digital networking can take a bit more effort, but so can any long-distance relationship. If you're in a position to get to know someone in person, evolve the relationship to meeting over coffee, sharing a meal, or attending a game together. In all cases, have your story ready, avoid excessive self-promotion, and try to keep your online presence and in-person persona aligned.

Getting Air Time in a Sea of Loud Voices

Not everyone is comfortable being the loudest person in the room. There are a few reasons for this: some may wait to share their thoughts due to their cultural orientation (those who were socialized with collectivist values), and some may do so because they're introverts and need time to process before sharing their opinion. I used to fall into the former category, and by the time I got to speak, the point had already been made. You can grow tired of trying to insert yourself between the louder voices that never seem to stop talking.

Keep an eye out for people who may want to speak but are being drowned out by louder voices. It might be that they're having a hard time entering the conversation. If you see this happening to a member of your team, you can connect one-on-one after the meeting and ask if they might want to have some built-in air time at the next meeting. Encourage them by letting them know that you value their opinions because of their good work, that you want to hear their insights, and that you appreciate their perspective—for example, you noticed their contributions in their previous project. But let them know that while you see their contributions, it may be beneficial for them to speak up once in a while in a group setting so that others in their project team can also hear their valuable thoughts. By doing so, you're not only giving them the safety net of supporting them in their work but also verbalizing to them that it will help their visibility in the organization.

Managing Zoom Fatigue

It's hard to be in front of a computer or laptop all day. Our eyes get tired and dry, and our heads start to hurt. Now, with the increase in on-camera meetings, we not only have to look at other faces onscreen, but we also have to look at ourselves for hours in the process. Staring at your own face and others all day long is a lot to ask of a human being—not to mention the extra attention required to interpret nuance, which can add to the overall brain fatigue. At the same time, we're quite often multitasking during meetings—checking email or planning our next task. It's a loaded situation. Mobility is also an issue. For the most part, we're stationary for long periods of time, unlike with phone calls, which can allow the movement that's critical for our overall health.

How do you avoid this uniquely twenty-first-century fatigue? Go on a "digital diet" once in a while, where you stay away from tablets, computers, and smartphones. Use the time to restore your in-person relationships and connect with your colleagues. When working, bring up alternative methods of meeting, limiting the number of on-camera meetings, or having a "break time" policy between them. On some platforms, you can remove self-view, so the group can still see you but you can't see yourself. If you find yourself having a difficult go with Zoom fatigue, speak up and suggest solutions. Chapter 9 will talk more about the importance of self-care in general.

Benefits of the Virtual Space

While there are drawbacks to the virtual space, there are also some benefits of this environment. Here are a few things that you can now do very easily since almost everyone has access to this technology:

- Attend a meeting with an online professional group associated with your interests without having to drive to a location after hours.

- Solve complex problems by joining online meetups that connect like-minded people in your industry.

- Expand beyond your current network. This can be just as effective as in-person networking, though it's perhaps harder to maintain effectively because of sheer numbers.

- Work from home more efficiently, giving you more time to spend with family and on other interests.

Best Practices for Virtual Interactions

Here are some guidelines to keep in mind when connecting with or building relationships with others in the virtual space:

- Make sure that your background is consistent with the professional image you want to convey. If your real background is less than ideal, use a blur of a simple background slide that's clean and pleasant.

- Watch your body language. Keep an eye on your upper body and how you're situated on the screen. Hold your body tall on screen, and make sure that the video camera isn't cutting off your body at the neck. I have heard from petite women that the virtual space has helped them gain a stronger presence. In person, they often felt small around taller men, and this affected their confidence because it felt like they were always looked down at.

- Lighting makes a huge difference; invest in a simple ring light and make sure your face is well lit and that the light isn't facing the camera.

- Speak clearly, and if people constantly tell you that they can't hear you well, it's a good idea to turn up your volume and practice in front of the camera first.

If both sides are working toward adapting to each other in any virtual communication encounter, the chances of a successful working relationship are higher. The adaptive mindset that each person brings will help create productive interactions and everyone will be giving each other more grace in this "new" setting.

If that's not the case, and you're the only one who recognizes how the cultural gaps are creating barriers to productivity, you can be the barometer for trying to bridge those gaps. Start engaging in the behaviors laid out above: inquire about how you can work together effectively and engage in ongoing cultural dialogue to determine how to best communicate.

There are many reasons why speaking up in a virtual setting is important. In the early days of a project team formation, you can set up a protocol about how you will address conflict issues in group meetings, and consider rotating the meeting facilitation role to give each member an opportunity to use their facilitation skills. By paying attention and making sure that *all* voices are heard in a meeting, you'll be creating an environment where even the quietest people feel like they're being valued.

There are definitely pros and cons to communicating in a digital space, but the goal is to try to create genuine connections with those around you, whether that means engaging in heart-to-heart leadership conversations with your team or finding ways to solicit fresh ideas for your business. Let the technology work *for* you instead of against you, and you'll find that virtual interactions can be just as productive as in-person ones.

Key Learning Points

- While digital platforms may be an efficient medium for connecting people when in-person meetings are not an option, keep in mind these environments also come with challenges:

  - Bias continues to exist in a virtual or hybrid environment and can be more challenging to identify and address. It's critical to be mindful of your audience.

  - Reading nuance, tonal changes, and body language can be more difficult to read. Gaps in communication can be amplified when you're working with high-context communication styles.

  - Zoom fatigue is a legitimate concern, and you should consider taking digital breaks periodically and engage in self-care practices.

- Be on the lookout for the less vocal or less emotionally expressive members of a group, affirming and validating their contributions. This is a powerful way to connect with others and stay attuned to those who may exhibit other communication styles.

9

LOOKING INWARD

Taking Care of Yourself

*Far too many of us have been taught to ignore
the emotional signs and push through what our
minds and bodies are telling us, and then to label
this self-denial as a sign of strength.*

—JENNY T. WANG, PhD, *Permission to Come Home*

When gold medal–winning gymnast Simone Biles decided to withdraw from the Olympic Games two years ago to attend to her mental health, it was a watershed moment to witness. The eyes of the world were on her at the 2020 Olympic Games with significant, well-deserved expectations. She was at the top of her game, had earned her stripes as a "GOAT" athlete, and was already a role model for many young girls. Yet she knew something wasn't quite right as she approached the 2021 Olympics; she was not in the best shape mentally and felt that she might hurt herself badly if she competed as well as diminish her team's overall chances of winning.

So often we push ourselves to excel when we are not feeling whole, either physically or mentally. We view indulgence in self-care as a weakness, a selfish endeavor that's a waste of time or money. And that view is often reinforced by others as well. When Biles decided to drop out of the Olympics, she was widely criticized and her decision was debated globally in the press. But she has remained steadfast that she made the right decision that day. In putting her mental health first, she was not only taking care of herself but also acknowledging that her state of mind could affect those around her negatively. She chose to prioritize her own health, despite what the world thought of her decision.

Growing up in immigrant families, many Asian Americans are familiar with the concept of pushing through the pain. They rarely gave themselves the space to consider their feelings or how their mental health is affecting them. They might not have felt it was okay to say that they needed some time to recharge. On top of that, in Asian American families, it's considered taboo to hang your "dirty laundry" out to dry in front of strangers. This is one of the reasons why the Western concept of talk therapy has not been widely utilized in the Asian American community and why many Asian parents never saw it as an option to turn to. Add to that, it is difficult to find culturally responsive counselors who can work effectively with the Asian American community. Many Asian Americans have never experienced their parents telling them they're tired after a long week or how they're dealing with the hurt from discriminatory comments they've received at their workplaces.

Moreover, many Asian American parents didn't always listen to their own bodies or attend to the pain and accumulated stress of working long, hard hours—even when they were at their breaking points. Many of them probably felt they had no choice. I remember watching my parents come home after long workdays six days a week with very little rest in between. I don't remember them complaining, either. I do remember when my mom collapsed one Sunday morning due to exhaustion and hit her forehead on the bathroom tiles. She had to go to the ER, but she still got up the next day and went right back to work.

Some Asian Americans have been socialized to not talk about hardships, having rarely heard their parents talk about their own experiences with racism. But I think there's space to share our vulnerability in the workplace as leaders for our team members. This takes real courage, but it's often necessary if we want to show our organizations who we truly are. It could be a path to healing together as a community.

While the concept of listening to your body and your mental needs might be foreign to you, it can create a cycle where you ignore what's happening for too long because you're so used to holding back your emotions or because enduring has become so normalized for you. But it's important to take a breath and check in with yourself. If you're not prioritizing your own health—whether that's physical or mental—then you're not showing up as your best, most authentic self. And as you've learned in previous chapters, the way to become a truly successful leader is by integrating the different parts of your self into your everyday life. This chapter will break down why it's so important to prioritize *you* and some tips for how to do that in a chaotic world.

How Are You Doing . . . Really?

Anyone who has traveled on an airplane has heard the preflight safety announcement about the oxygen mask: you must put yours on first before you can help others. And there's truth to this in all scenarios. When you're responsible for others, whether family or colleagues, you can't give your best unless you're taking care of yourself mentally and physically first. This is especially true when you're raised in a culture that's teaching you the opposite from a young age. From one angle, it seems so selfish, doesn't it? It's harder to prioritize your mental health when you've watched your parents endure hardship, long hours, microaggressions from others, and depression, often without complaint and without relief. So let's talk about some of the ways you can start to examine your mental health to ensure that you're in a position to give your best to those around you.

Ask yourself: Am I feeling the fullness of someone who is engaged with the world in a way that makes me proud, happy, and satisfied? If you're feeling the opposite, it might be time to reach out for help. Ignoring early signs of trouble is the surest way to have a problem grow more significant as time goes on. This is where it's time to break the stigma of mental health that many Asian Americans grew up with and go see a counselor or therapist. If you broke your leg, you'd go see a doctor immediately—and the mind isn't any different. If you're having symptoms of emotional or mental fatigue, depression, or persistent insomnia, see a doctor. You have a right, and a responsibility, to feel well.

The first step in all of this is to learn how to check in with yourself, and to do it often; to look deeper inside and ask yourself: Is my cup half full or half empty? Am I pouring out my resources to others from an empty cup? And if it is nearing depletion, what are the steps I can take to learn how to fill it?

Unpacking Pressure and Achievement

It's easy for me to tell you to prioritize yourself and that it's okay to ask for help, but I understand that this is easier said than done. One Asian cultural value is prizing educational achievement and hard work. For many Asian Americans, that means that their parents were pushing them from a young age to excel. It's such a common refrain that they never stop to think about what they actually want or how it makes them feel. And that pressure to achieve doesn't end with graduating cum laude: they move into their careers with the same pressure to be a reliable producer for the company and to move up as quickly as possible so they can make their families proud.

Have you ever stepped back and asked yourself why you're doing the work you do and how you feel about it? Do you enjoy it? Does it fulfill you beyond the satisfaction of achievement for achievement's sake? These are important questions to ask yourself about a career that you'll devote forty years or more of your life to.

It's crucial to start doing the work of unpacking *how* and *why* you ended up in the position you're in. Even if you pursued this career initially because of academic or familial pressures, what do you love about it now? What value does it bring to your life?

If you can identify and isolate reasons that are not tied to your familial or cultural expectations, you can start letting go of the fear and shame that's tied up in failure.

Overcoming a Guilt- or Shame-Based Culture

When you're from a culture that has an underlying layer of shame, it can be extra difficult to reach out and ask for help. And that's what many Asian Americans are dealing with: the idea that if they make a mistake or something goes wrong, they'll have to deal with the aftermath. They're not just letting *themselves* down, they're disappointing their entire family and community. This can feel devastating, especially when they know there are high expectations for them.

In the workplace, the reality that you often find yourself the only Asian in the room can exacerbate this dynamic, as you feel the pressure of doing right by representing other Asian Americans well. Your performance is reflective not only of yourself but of your *entire cultural community*, which can add to your levels of stress and expectation. If you're feeling overwhelmed, it's no wonder! But just know: you're not alone in this, and as difficult as it may be, divorcing yourself from the shame is the first step toward removing some of that unnecessary stress.

Recognizing the Stress You Carry

We often think of stress as something that lives solely in our heads, but this isn't true. I learned this the hard way when I was going through grief counseling after my mother passed away. I had been pushing through my pain in order to deal with all the travel and work ahead of me, and I hadn't had the chance to properly understand what her loss meant and how it was affecting my psyche.

Steven Porges's polyvagal theory shows that we carry the stress, pressure, and pain we experience in our bodies. His theory introduced a new understanding of trauma and recovery, and it has helped me understand and manage the loss of my mother. It's also helped me be mindful (and not ignore) the daily stresses I encounter in my work activities. Now, I try to determine where the stress is sitting in my body and how that affects me. When I recognize myself hitting a wall when I experience something extremely difficult, it helps me to recenter and try to get back to a place of safety.

Deb Dana, a clinical social worker, applied this theory further and shared that the ventral side of the vagus nerve helps us feel safe, show up, communicate, and connect with others. She calls the ventral vagal state *home*: a place of safety where we feel connected and want to be most of the time. This all stems from the flight or fight response that helps us mobilize and survive in dangerous environments. If we cannot fight or take flight, the dorsal side of the vagus nerve has us shut down, collapse, or go numb in order to protect us.

If you're operating every hour of the day in a state of fight or flight, it's easy to see that you might hit that dorsal vagal state in order to protect yourself. This is when you might feel that sensation of being depleted at the end of the workday.

It's important to recognize when these moments happen. For me, they usually occur when I hear some difficult news. I can trace it back to the time my mom had to be admitted to the ER from the rehab center. I didn't understand the impact of the shock and grief right away, but for months, perhaps a year, I continued to feel the weight of something heavy in my very being. It wasn't until I started getting grief counseling a good two years after her passing that I started to face the weight I was carrying inside me.

Ask yourself:

- When do I feel the most stress or anxiety?

- Where do I carry stress in my body?

- When I feel that stress, what do I do next?

Not All Stress Is Created Equal

Imagine you're about to give a big presentation and your stomach is full of butterflies. Or you're about to go into an important meeting with your boss and your chest feels tight. We've all felt that before, and while sometimes it can add to our nerves, overall it's actually keeping us more alert and focused.

Not all stress is bad stress. Sometimes it can actually be helpful, alerting us when a moment is important or when we need to pay more specific attention to what's happening around us. These short spurts of stress—known as acute, or short-lived stress—can help motivate and inspire you, focus your energy, and keep you alert. They can also help you develop habits and coping skills for more stressful periods in life. This is something that everyone feels, and it's completely normal.

Anand Chokkalingam, head of Real World Evidence Virology at Gilead Sciences, has a specific stress management practice he uses right before he gives important presentations. Assuming he's fully prepared for the presentation, he says that the stress he typically feels is good stress; it's almost always just anticipation. To address this, he works on modulating his breathing and heart rate and taking several slow, deep cleansing breaths. He says, "Of course, I'll also review my slides, and I'll visualize myself giving the talk in my mind's eye and visualize it finishing well." For Anand, what keeps him going is focusing on the lasting impact his team's research is having on human lives, how he gets to learn something every day, and the enjoyment he gets from working with a great team of scientists.

The takeaway is that there's good stress, bad stress, and chronic stress. Good stress can keep you motivated, whereas bad stress, if left unchecked, can lead to chronic stress. When stress is chronic or there's no relief, you end up living with an ongoing sense of dread that can cause long-term challenges to productivity. Many of us experienced this during the pandemic, when it felt like there was no end in sight to this "new normal" we were all stuck in. The trick is to check in with yourself: What kind of stress are you experiencing, and is it temporary? Or are you like Anand, and your stress is actually anticipation that can be harnessed to motivate and inspire you to do a greater good?

Taking Care of Yourself before Going "On Stage" and Managing Other Stressors

When I started presenting in front of audiences multiple times a week, I made it a practice to ask for thirty minutes of quiet time in a side room. Once, when I was speaking at a conference held at a college campus, there was no "speaker room" for me. So, instead, I snuck into a stall of the ladies' room and prayed to prepare myself mentally to meet my audience. Not only did that help me focus on the audience (and not my nerves), it also grounded me so I could recognize the greater purpose that I was there to accomplish. The few times I wasn't able to have this quiet time before going live, I was usually flustered and got caught up and distracted by the people, the crowds, the questions, and so on. I realized early on that I need to prioritize taking care of myself in order to perform at a top level, but that only I could identify what would work for me.

Here are a few ways to start taking care of yourself proactively:

- **If you feel like you're stressed, identify the source.** Practice being present and centering yourself in times of extreme stress. Where is it coming from? How can you recognize the source and begin to mitigate it?

- **Make your physical health a priority.** If you work in a sedentary job, get up every two meetings or Zoom calls to take a short walk around the floor or block. If you can take a walk in the park during your lunch hour, that could be helpful too.

- **Consider what you put *in* your body.** Try drinking water right when you wake up, and eating foods that make you feel good. If you feel good in your body, it often helps with how you feel in your mind as well.

- **Train for the work you want to do**. Always seeking out new ways to learn can keep your mind sharp and your creativity invigorated. Attend at least one training a year to refine something for your work or learn something new from an expert. This will keep you in a learning mode.

- **Seek help or support from others.** If there's a job task that you know you can delegate, do it. Also know that you can't do it alone, especially if you're experiencing extreme stress for extended periods of time and you feel like you're spiraling. Get the support you need; it's not shameful to ask for help.

Jane's Healthy Practices

Here are a few practices that I've learned over the years to help me reduce stress in my workplace:

- **Reduce your intake of things that trigger anxiety or stress where you can.** Limit social media and news to a defined period in the day. Take a "digital fast" from technology at least once a week.

- **Have things near your desk that bring a smile to your face, or better, make you laugh.** Display a cherished family photo, a quote, a memento from a trip you took with your buddies, an object that evokes a childhood memory, a bobble head, or anything that makes you feel grounded.

- **Learn to listen to your body, especially when you feel anxiety start to take hold.** It's easy to miss things or misinterpret what others say when you're chronically stressed. Communicate carefully with yourself and ask: Who or what is contributing to this feeling? What is my intention?

- **Stay in regular contact with advisors and mentors who are life-giving and not life-draining.** Add them to your growing network. (Refer back to chapter 7.)

There's no right or wrong way to take care of yourself: these are simple practices that have worked for me and my clients that I try to implement in my daily life. I've found that no matter what's going on at work, I can deal with the stresses in my life when I'm connected to my family and friends and checking in with myself. Many times, this has meant leaving space in my life for solitude and journaling. Your own practices might be different, but the core message is the same: listen to what your body and mind need and prioritize those needs as much as you can, taking breaks as you need to. You have important work ahead of you to accomplish!

Meeting the Needs of the Adoptee Community

Hollee A. McGinnis, PhD, MSW, remembers working on her senior thesis on the racial and ethnic identity of other college-aged Korean American women who were adopted like herself. Two years after college when she cofounded Also-Known-As, Inc. (AKA) in 1996 with Peter Savasta, Joy Lieberthal-Rho, Mea Han Nelson Fajardo, and Lynn Richards, there was no easy way to connect with other adult Korean American adoptees. Hollee says, "At the Asian American Heritage festival, I was literally walking around Lincoln Center asking people if they knew where to track down adoptees."

For Hollee and many transracial adoptees, growing up in a family that looks different from them is fraught with emotions, as adoptees have to navigate two families—one known and the other typically not known. Hollee was adopted into an Irish Catholic family in Westchester County, New York, and there was a time when it was hard for her to bring up being Korean because her white parents did not know how to acknowledge the racism she experienced.

AKA is a community that seeks to empower through community with other adult adoptees, bridge cultural gaps with adoptees' birth cultures, transform racism, and serve through programs like mentoring adopted children and teens and workshops for adoptive parents. Although the first members of AKA were mainly Korean, the group was always intended to be inclusive, and recently the number of Chinese adoptees has grown significantly. Hollee, now an assistant professor at the Virginia Commonwealth University School of Social Work, continues to serve in an advisory capacity to AKA and has launched an initiative to map the life course of adoption to understand how adoptees are aging, the effects of cumulative stressors, and how connections to other adoptees impact their lives.

Advocating for Yourself and Others

Others might not know about or might overlook the challenges you face unless you talk about it. Because many of us have been conditioned *not* to talk about this at home, it can be difficult to acknowledge, especially out loud. But as with any situation in your life, if you need help and are struggling, reach out and ask for help.

Help can manifest in many different ways. When it comes to overwhelming stress at work that's affecting your mental health, I suggest you begin with your mentor or the support group you've built for yourself. These are people who can help you find your way back to the path—or perhaps to a new path, if that's what in order. If you need professional support, the next step would be to consult a professional therapist or social worker.

When it comes to advocating for your needs in the workplace, here are three tips for moving forward:

- **Understand your value to the organization and make sure that people around you are aware of it.** When you know what you bring to the table you will have more conviction about your marketability and be in a better position to ask for what you need (whether that's a lateral role or project, a raise, or time off).

- **Tap into your company's benefits for employee well-being.** Many organizations have mental health initiatives that you can access. See if their resources might be helpful to you. And if you need to take a leave of absence from work to address your mental health, this is often covered by your employer.

- **Rehearse difficult conversations ahead of time.** If you need to have a courageous conversation with someone in your organization (including your leadership), plan it out. Rehearse what you're going to say so that you're best equipped to inform others about what you need to be successful.

Of course there are resources out there for you to draw on, from mental health initiatives to medical professionals, but the first step starts with *you*. Only you can know what's going on inside of you, so don't be afraid to advocate for what you need.

Reflection Questions

- What might be keeping you from taking a break?

- What aspects of your family experiences or upbringing have helped you manage stress?

- What is your favorite way to rest and recharge your batteries?

Reflect on the questions you just answered. What did you take away from them? Were there valuable learnings gained from your family that have been helpful? Pay attention to your thoughts—the actual words and the language that you use when you're overtaxing yourself—as they may indicate how you think generally about taking care of your well-being (or not). Inspecting your self-talk and attitudes can give you insight into how you internalize what you have learned.

Reframing Disempowering Self-Talk

Can you relate to any of the following "inner voice" statements?

- *Wellness and mental health all sounds good, but in my company prioritizing my needs would be seen as weak and might be held against me.*

- *I'm a doer who gets things done. Who's going to do it as well as I can?*

- *What if the guy I'm competing with for a promotion doesn't take time off and I'm seen as the one who needs more help than others? Am I going to be pigeonholed as a slacker or someone who's less motivated?*

- *If we don't deliver, we're going to lose credibility with our biggest client.*

Now try reframing those "what ifs" into healthy thoughts like the following:

- *I'll hit a wall this year if I don't take a break pretty soon. I'll plan out my work so that natural breaks are incorporated into my deliverables, and I'm going to work with my team to develop a realistic project plan.*

- *I've been on the go for six months straight. It's time for a meaningful break, without being on the road, so I can plan for next year's priorities. It's okay to say no to clients who are unable to wait for us.*

- *My job as the head of this team is to equip my team to succeed in their own way. I will trust them with this and support them with the guardrails they need.*

Now try filling in examples from your own experience below.

DISEMPOWERING SELF-TALK	REFRAMED THOUGHT
What if the whole project goes south?	*Part of my job as a leader is to develop my people so that I can delegate to them when I need to. We've got a lot of talent in our team!*
Who's going to do it as well as I can?	

Tapping into Cultural Resilience Practices

*If you remember the resilience of your
ancestors, you will never be conquered.*

—POTRI RANKA MANIS, visual artist,
founder of Kinding Sindaw Dance Company

It can be easy to blame our mental health issues on our families or cultural values, but of course it's more nuanced than that. And there are aspects of our family and cultural experiences (often from our countries of origin) that can help us deal with and respond to the challenges we encounter, if we allow ourselves to see them.

Cultural resilience refers to a culture's capacity to maintain and develop cultural practices and identity when they face adversity. As an example, cultural resilience made a difference when Hurricane Hugo devastated the US Virgin Islands in 1990, and many people lost access to electricity and gas. They were able to revert to cooking over coal in a coal pot, a tradition dating from the 1800s. The islands were a subject of the Smithsonian's Festival of American Folklife program that year, with the coal pot as a central theme both as a cooking utensil and a symbol of resilience.

When I was younger and confronted with a difficult task, my mom would often tell me to *"chahm euh,"* a Korean phrase that loosely translates to "push through the pain." When I was going through a rough patch in college, that phrase, delivered with a sincere heart, helped me to endure. The concept of persisting through hardship and uncertainty was something my mother understood well, having grown up in wartime Korea. While grinning and bearing it doesn't apply in all situations, knowing that the phrase helped her, coupled with her tender words of comfort reminding me that "we come from strong stock" and the food she sent, lifted my spirits!

What did you see modeled in your family when adversity hit? Maybe you grew up going to a place of worship, and prayer or meditation was an important part of your life. If this is the case, what practices did you learn as a child that might strengthen you now? Do you find comfort in meditation or in prayer? Sometimes even the act of sitting quietly and reflecting can have lasting effects. What did your parents, grandparents, or extended family members do to relieve a difficult situation and help a family member in crisis? Family and community support was a big source of strength for my family when I was growing up in Korea. My extended family came to support us if a family member was ill. Tapping into the collective ways my family has positively affected my relationship to my mental health has been really helpful when it comes to prioritizing my own needs. What are some ways your own family has modeled positive behavior around mental health?

Practicing Self-Compassion

For some people, it might seem intuitive that they need to care for their mind and body in order to feel balanced and fully present in their life. But if you were raised in a shame-based culture that prioritizes achievement and a strong work ethic over leisure or self-care and where talk therapy was a foreign concept, you might not even be aware of how much you're carrying at any given time. If you want to see results in your career and lead others with empathy, then you have to bring your best, more authentic self to the workplace. It's important to get in touch with yourself—both physically and mentally—since your state of being is directly tied to how you show up in your life. And while that may not happen overnight, you can start to be conscious of it. The way to do that is to take care of yourself, remain in the present, and advocate for your needs. Doing so will not only make you a more grounded leader, but will serve as a model for your team members. If you destigmatize caring for your own needs, they will also give themselves permission to do so. This is the mark of a true leader: being compassionate for others *and* yourself in this constantly changing world.

Fast-forward to October 2023. Simone Biles came back after a two-year hiatus to bring home four more gold medals at the World Championships in 2023. That makes her the most decorated gymnast of all time, among both men and women. Her mental health break made her even stronger. Imagine what it could do for you.

Key Points for Reflection

- Begin with an honest self-assessment: *How am I really doing? What unhealthy behaviors and attitudes have I accepted, even if born from well-meaning expectations? What does my self-talk sound like on an average day? If it's negative, how can I reframe it to foster a healthier mindset?*

- If you've been conditioned to view self-care as a form of weakness, what's your takeaway from Simone Biles's hiatus and subsequent return to glory?

- Try to distinguish between good, bad, and chronic stress, with an awareness of the toll that the latter takes not just on your mind but on your body as well.

- Your gameplan moving forward should be two-fold: 1) identify and eliminate triggers that take you to an unproductive place, and 2) incorporate healthy behaviors into your life, such as reaching out to others, delegating tasks, or engaging with trusted mentors and advisors, among others.

- Try out at least one new way of recharging your batteries.

10

ENGAGING ADVOCATES AND LEVERAGING FEEDBACK

The most fundamental thing about leadership is to have the humility to continue to get feedback and to try to get better— because your job is to try to help everybody else get better.

—JIM YONG KIM, cofounder, Partners
in Health; former World Bank president

Whenever I watch reality shows like *Chopped* or *Shark Tank*, it reminds me of how powerful feedback can be. While constructive comments can be hard for the contestants to take immediately after a performance (especially if they don't get selected!), you see the value of a judge's point of view on full display. Win or lose, the contestants walk away with some meaningful feedback.

But, as you can see from some of these episodes, learning how to accept feedback gracefully is a skill that needs to be developed. During the pandemic, my daughter once overheard my husband on the phone giving specific, direct feedback to his colleague about how a project was handled. She later approached me with a look of concern on her face and stated, "Wow, Daddy sounded angry!" Because of the direct nature of the call, she thought that my husband was upset. But in reality, it was an everyday business conversation—giving routine feedback to an associate about how he might enhance his approach. It wasn't punitive at all, and his colleague welcomed the feedback, as he was eager to improve before his next presentation. It was the first time my daughter realized that in the corporate workplace you sometimes need to communicate feedback explicitly in order to improve a process.

As we've discussed, networking and creating connections are crucial when it comes to advancing in your organization. One valuable output from those relationships is feedback and understanding *how* to engage your advocates in a way that creates iterative change, innovative ideas, and productive conversations. In this chapter, I'll break down what it means to leverage your community to the best of your ability while continuing to grow in your leadership by applying feedback from others. I'll also give you a few specific ways to share your leadership model with others, which will help you begin to implement your new vision.

Sharing Your Vision and Leadership Model

Now that you've developed a leadership approach you feel good about, it's time to share it with people who will help you continue to refine it. If you don't, important stakeholders will miss the benefit of knowing your vision. They also won't be able to help you improve your vision or advance your goals. If you're going through my firm's leadership accelerator programs, we will guide you through the process of sharing your model and work on feedback with your accountability group. However, if you're picking up this book on your own, you can find someone to share your work with who will give you concrete external perspective. Either way, it's essential to consider who you're going to bring into your leadership journey and how you're going to apply the feedback you receive.

Start by sharing your leadership model with one or two trusted advisors who have your back. If it makes you more comfortable, start by choosing one person *outside* of your company before taking it to someone on the inside. But it will eventually be beneficial for you to identify a trusted work colleague with whom you can discuss it. They will know the mission, the business environment, and the goals of the company better than an outsider will.

Whom should you select first? That's an important person to get right.

Perhaps it's a previous manager with whom you have a great relationship, or a mentor or trusted senior leader who first showed you how to decipher the intricate politics of the organization. Pick someone who knows you well and has enough experience with you to provide feedback; they should know how you typically think and work, have some experience interacting with you and seeing you demonstrate your leadership skills, and have visibility into your strengths and areas for improvement. Then, after you've met with them, vetted the model, and shared your vision, you can begin to consider if and when you might share your model with your direct manager or leadership.

If you're hesitant to share this work with someone in your organization, I understand. It's natural to feel cautious when you're preparing to share something so personal and important with a colleague or a mentor. But I hope that after reading this chapter you'll feel a little more comfortable sharing your model with a trusted colleague and that you'll take away a few solid tactics for fully leveraging these meaningful relationships.

Preparing to Share Your Vision with Management

Before you invite your leaders to weigh in, here are some questions to consider:

- What is your manager's attitude toward diversity and difference and their level of understanding?

- What language do they use to talk about difference?

- Do they fully embrace the importance of diversity, equity, and inclusion (DEI)?

- Do they understand what your cultural perspective and identity bring to the organization?

- When you discuss your ideas and vision with them, what language do you use? Do you use DEI language, or would it be better to position your model from a business-aligned perspective?

These are important considerations because understanding your leaders' current mindsets will help you determine how to approach them. Their mindset toward difference will inform what they see and care about. Thinking back to chapter 3, where do you think they might be in the five orientations of the Intercultural Development Continuum? Could they be in a Minimization mindset? Will they be able to meet you where you are? There's no way for you to know this at the outset, of course, but you can imagine that unless your manager is coming from an Acceptance or Adaptation (both multicultural views) mindset, their approach may very well be "Do it the way I want you to do it!"—meaning they just want the work to get done and they're not thinking beyond that; your cultural experiences don't matter to them. They're not being mean or intentionally insensitive to you; it's just how they think. They're simply not ready to consider the possibilities that come from a more multicultural mindset; hence, they might not be able to fully grasp what you're trying to tell them. If, on the other hand, you go in by showing how your approach will help the organization achieve some of its business or future organizational goals, then you're more likely to get a positive reaction.

After all, here's what your senior business leaders most care about:

- How you'll get the tasks done and the outcomes

- Your deliverables and how they impact the greater goals of the company

- How effectively and efficiently you can solve (with your team) the pressing problems that your group or department is tasked with

By focusing your approach on how your leadership model and new approaches will enable you to get this work done more effectively, you have a stronger chance of having your vision accepted and supported, as you'll clearly be contributing to the leaders' priorities too.

Now, if you're already fairly certain you have a senior leader or manager who is ready to receive some of the innovative thinking in your leadership model, then you might be in a better position right off the bat.

Sharing with Team Members One-on-One

When you're ready to share your model with your direct reports, you'll want to come at it from a different angle. You're now coming from the perspective of being vulnerable and sharing something that's important to you so that you can create the conditions to bring out the best in your team. It's also an opportunity for you to show some vulnerability (this is especially important if you haven't yet had a lot of experience engaging with your team).

Here are some tips on how to go about sharing your model with individual team members. Keep in mind that the underlying question is: What do they need from you in order to succeed?

- Integrate the conversation into your existing one-on-one "how are we working together" conversations where you're already sharing feedback.

- Start by sharing your vision for your team and then ask them what kind of leadership they need, taking their comments into consideration.

- Share what you hope to achieve with your leadership model and the cultural values that you have reflected on that bring out your unique style.

Also, consider how their perspective could affect your approach. If a report says to you, "I need very explicit, clear, direct feedback from management," and you're used to using a softer touch, then you run the risk of being perceived as too weak or ineffective. So, instead, try to engage them in a dialogue by saying something like, "This is how I lead, and I am usually more productive when I can bring more of this approach to my day to day. Let's talk about how we can make it more productive for both of us. How can we design how we work together so that you have the input that you need from me to do your job and you also see where I'm coming from?" By stating this, you're demonstrating that you're willing to meet them partway.

It's a good idea to tie this critical conversation to your desire to help them achieve success with the goals they care about. This could be a chance to share a little more about yourself and what your intentions are too.

Next, when you bring the model to your entire team collectively (versus one-on-one), you can use a similar approach. However, the difference between sharing your model with a manager and sharing it with your team is that you're coming up with a *group* version of how you can all work together as opposed to an individual approach. You'll need to consider how you can design the most helpful plan for your entire group, especially if members of your team are coming from a different cultural perspective.

Sharing with a Group

When working in a diverse team, we have to intentionally design how we work together, because we bring all sorts of differences to the table—our conflict style and feedback preferences, our brainstorming styles, and our motivations. While you may think your style is just common sense and that most people will be okay with it, some may not. Time and again, I've seen multicultural teams fizzle out and get demotivated because their styles of engagement—which are always simmering under the surface—are rarely discussed until a blowup occurs. In high-performing teams, each person must take time to work on their own development *and* the entire team's development.

If you're a more low-key leader and effective at engaging others, that's fine and good. However, what if others don't like that approach? No matter how authentic your approach is for you, think about the implications of it for other people. Also consider how to get your team to shift their thinking so they can see the value of what you're bringing. Don't be naïve or make assumptions about how they want to be led by you. Depending on the situation, you may need to adapt how you communicate initially and meet them where they are until you can create a new precedent.

The goal of a group dialogue is to make it easier for everyone to participate in the discussion and feel that their thoughts, opinions, and insights have been heard. Don't expect people to know how to operate in a multicultural setting. One way to work on this is to send out a draft agenda before the meeting so that you get written input ahead of time from all of your team members. This will "prewire" the meeting some and prepare the team for what's to come. You can also allow for side conversations, which will make people feel more open in the meeting.

Perceptions matter. If you're ready to unveil your leadership approach and vision with your direct reports, here are some guidelines to increase your chances of being well received:

- Before you share your model with your team, you need to consider *how you're perceived by them.* Even if what you're doing is working so far, they may be expecting something else, so it's helpful to recognize their expectations—you may need to shift something!

  The goal of a group dialogue is to make it easier for everyone to participate in the discussion and feel that their thoughts, opinions, and insights have been heard.

- Work on building strong relationships among your team members by discussing how you work together now and how you want to work together going forward.

Team development doesn't happen without team members first recognizing that there are differences at play (including cultural differences and preferences) that might get in the way, and then figuring out a way to work together that suits everyone. Creating a high-performing team requires knowing and explicitly communicating to the group each team member's different strengths and perspectives in order to better leverage them for new ideas or solutions to difficult problems. Whenever possible, emphasize the importance of varied approaches and validate the differences within the team. Each member needs to be working toward a mutually defined goal. This might mean adapting your leadership approach and defining norms (together as a group) so that you're considering each team member and their unique point of view.

Exchanging Feedback with Grace

While feedback can provide vital information about your effectiveness, taking in the new information and responding to it gracefully can be difficult, as it requires a level of vulnerability. How can you listen to what someone is telling you without citing a reason for your actions and not immediately jumping to a solution?

The leadership story that follows is a reminder that when you attempt something important and fail at it, it's tempting to run away or avoid dealing with the associated feelings of shame. But with the right advocate or manager, you can recover and persevere.

Turning Feedback into a Lifelong Mutual Mentoring Relationship

When Anand Chokkalingam, the head of Real World Evidence Virology at Gilead introduced in chapter 9, was a PhD candidate at the University of Maryland, he reached out to Dr. Ann Hsing, then a senior investigator and epidemiologist at the National Cancer Institute.

Anand needed help with his dissertation and Ann was someone whose work he admired. He "cold emailed" her after finding her email address in one of her research papers. Anand doesn't know exactly when she became his mentor, but their relationship has lasted over twenty-four years. There were many times when Ann's feedback was really tough to take, but Anand always knew she was coming from a good place.

The most challenging project that Anand worked on involved understanding the impact of prostate cancer in West Africa. The project was such an abstract concept and he didn't quite know how to move it forward. He was floundering in the early stages of the research, and Ann could see it. Anand remembers multiple times when she took him aside and said very directly, "This isn't going very well, is it?" He knew that Ann's comments were meant to be supportive, however. He shares, "Knowing that she had my best interest in mind, it started to break down a bit of the shame I had felt. It was beneficial for me to hear her voicing those words. Shame is a funny thing. A previous iteration of Anand would have thought: 'I'm so ashamed; I can't face her anymore. . . . I have to run away.' *I couldn't run away from it, though.* It was clear to me that she genuinely cared about my development as a researcher. That made me press on."

Anand could always count on Ann for timely, insightful feedback that brought clarity to his projects; he knew that she absolutely had his best interests at heart. Later, he was able to assist her as well. "I wrote her a recommendation to Stanford when she was considering a position there, and my parents helped her get settled in a new home when she relocated to the Bay Area. It was satisfying to see our relationship come full circle."

The exchange of feedback is a vital piece of any successful team, creating a chain of connection between leaders and their team members. Therefore, it's important to understand how to give successful feedback *and* how to take it in a graceful way. This is especially true when it comes to sharing your leadership model as well—you want to be open to the feedback you receive without shoving your agenda onto a team that might not be ready to hear it yet.

Giving Feedback

When giving feedback to someone, be as clear as you can. If you're not, the recipient might not fully understand your intentions or connect to what they're doing well or what they need to improve upon. Write down your feedback first if you suspect that the content might be particularly sensitive for the receiver to hear. Be clear about your goals for giving the feedback, and then articulate them to the employee as well.

Also consider the timing and format of your feedback. For example, if one of your employees has just given a presentation, deliver any critical feedback as soon as you can so you can capture the emotions of and impact on the audience. If you're providing feedback about a twenty-page strategic plan, consider a working session where you can provide one-on-one feedback that shows the recipient what worked well. This can be a two-way exchange for asking clarifying questions and helping them plan their next steps. The goal of that session would be to improve and refine. Another kind of feedback could be periodic observation over a span of time. No matter the goal or format, your intent should be to help, improve, educate, or praise, with specific examples.

Receiving Feedback

When receiving feedback, the one rule of thumb is to receive it with gratitude. Feedback helps you refine your skills and clarify your goals, and your attitude toward receiving feedback can reflect your willingness to learn and grow.

Honoring Feedback from Experienced Colleagues

Marshall Cho, introduced in chapter 4, remembers his early days of teaching in the Teach For America program in the Bronx. "There was this teacher, Mr. Hernandez, who was actually a licensed doctor, and he took a liking to me. He used to do home visits to the students, and he advised me early on at the school that home visits were important if I wanted to be effective with the students. He took me around with him, and I saw him in action." This feedback showed Marshall that he needed to be intentional about doing the outreach to connect with his students outside of the classroom.

Instead of ignoring the direct feedback he was receiving from Mr. Hernandez, Cho chose to honor his advice. "After the incident on my first day as a teacher [when the students tried to walk out of the classroom], the next weekend I did home visits to their family homes. It was eye-opening to visit their homes and meet their family members. In one particular visit, the student opened the door and was shocked that I showed up. When I went back to school on Monday after I started doing home visits, word had gotten out that, 'If you mess with Mr. Cho, he'll show up at your door on Saturday morning.'" By taking the advice and guidance of a more senior administrator who understood the cultural norms, Cho was better able to gain control of his classroom and create valuable relationships—and build credibility—with his students.

Like Marshall, be open to help from those with more contextual knowledge than you, and then genuinely listen and apply their feedback. Remain curious, ask probing questions to better understand what you're hearing, and ask for clarity if you need. Feedback from a well-intentioned person provides a lot of important information, even if it's constructive. Practice affirming self-talk when you hear feedback that you disagree with in the moment; remind yourself that you are valuable and your inherent worth is not dependent on one person's feedback. Regardless, try to keep your emotions in check, and then, if you need to, sit on it overnight before you respond or take action. The next day, after you have taken it in and asked some follow-up questions to get more details, you can map out a plan to determine how you should proceed.

Whether you're sharing your leadership model for the first time or trying out new ways to give and receive feedback, the efforts you make can strengthen your work relationships over the long term. By soliciting input from people you trust, you will gain more clarity about your goals and new perspectives on how to approach your most critical business challenges. As an added perk, when you are known for welcoming a culture of healthy feedback in your teams, you create a learning environment where individuals are encouraged to continuously grow. Over time, you'll build a culture of safety that enables people to take risks and ultimately fosters more authenticity in the workplace.

Key Learning Points

- Congrats! It's time for you to start sharing the work you've been doing here. How might you go about initiating a conversation with your leader? What will you need to prepare for that conversation? How will you frame the conversation?

- It's always beneficial to consult with someone you trust within your company who is aware of the actual business context before you share your model with your manager.

- The key skill in receiving feedback from managers is, *again*, to know your audience. In this case, that means being aware of both their mindset in terms of responding to difference and their business-aligned goals and priorities. Speak to their priorities as you share your intentions, and frame your goals alongside what they care about too.

- Likewise, when giving feedback as a manager or leader, it's critical to account for the communication styles and feedback preferences of each member of your team. Consider the appropriate time and format for delivering your feedback, and always approach it from a position of offering support, constructive questions, and a growth mindset. Be clear about your goals, and demonstrate openness to hearing your direct report's perspective and answering their follow-up questions.

11

STEPPING ONTO
THE GLOBAL STAGE

*If you want to reach consumers in different parts
of the world, speak to them in a way they understand.*

—MARIEKE DE MOOIJ, global marketing
and advertising expert and author

The world is changing. Despite the multitude of challenges over the past few years, the IMF reported that the Asia–Pacific region will account for 70 percent of global growth this year. More than 50 percent of the world's middle class lives in Asia. Though China's rate of growth slowed during Covid and is struggling to return to its accelerated pre-pandemic state, the majority of the world's semiconductors are manufactured there, as well as in Taiwan and South Korea. The region will drive much of the global economic growth in the next decade, and there will be countless opportunities for you to play a role in this market.

In their book *International Management Behavior*, Henry Lane and Martha Maznevski write, "In the 21st century, being a global leader is no longer a nice-to-have capability, it is a must-have for those who want to create value for their organizations." Given its rate of change and the sheer cultural diversity of the

Asia–Pacific region, it requires leaders who are capable of navigating many different styles of doing business. We still need *people* to handle the complex business of selling, marketing, communicating, and negotiating in a global space. It will take both a global mindset *and* cultural fluency in leadership behaviors to work effectively in this global business environment. You'll need a willingness to set aside existing frameworks and create pathways where none existed before. This chapter asks: What role could you play in Asia, and in other global markets, in this interconnected environment where change is the common denominator? How could your cultural experiences be an asset to leverage for the future of business and society?

Are You a Global Leader?

As people who have often straddled the challenge of "living in two worlds" and navigating in a dominant culture, Asian American leaders and other multicultural, multiracial professionals have skills that may be valuable in today's unpredictable terrain. If you've been socialized within a dominant culture that may have overlooked your potential, you have an edge when confronting new cultures and adapting to different ways of being. You also bring an alternative point of view, a different vantage point: you are used to working with difference and navigating challenging environments. This is what a true global leader needs—the resilience, cultural fluency, and willingness to do what it takes to work harmoniously with people different from themselves.

If you've taken the work in this book seriously, you could be in an especially good position to work on a global level.

Culturally Fluent Leaders Are Hard to Come By

Not everyone is in this position, however. Through my business, I've found that leaders who are equipped to navigate the conflicts of global hybrid teams while skillfully working in an international business environment are extremely rare. Many people overestimate their ability to navigate differences, especially if they haven't done the work of confronting their own bias. This is certainly true in the United States, but when it comes to working in Asian countries, challenges with cultural fluency are magnified. Understanding the high-context, relationship-driven cultures of many Asian countries is difficult if you've been steeped in a more direct, task-oriented business culture. If you're not doing the work of understanding and unpacking these unfamiliar cultures, you'll likely face challenges in this new environment.

While doing leadership research in China, I met a headhunter who told me he was perplexed by how impatient US CEOs were. They wanted to find local country heads as efficiently as possible. "US executives decide after a fifty-minute conversation whether a candidate would be the right fit for their company, assuming that bilingual skills and education are sufficient for effective local leadership for a multinational company. They discuss business but spend very little time getting to know the candidate personally. I have to remind them that they should consider taking the final candidate for a bike ride in the park and perhaps even a leisurely dinner together on a different day." Often, they were ready to extend a job offer after one round of interviews. The headhunter reflected that, "Here, they would spend a whole week with that individual, including multiple meetings over a period of time to get better acquainted with the potential hire."

Similarly, my team and I went to Asia to facilitate an onsite, three-day "Local to Global Leadership Accelerator" leadership program for a global consumer products company. There, we worked with thirty senior leaders from their Asian locations. (The program brought together a cohort of senior leaders from Vietnam, Malaysia, South Korea, Japan, the Philippines, and Thailand. We later held a separate program for the Greater China region.) One leader from the program confided in us during lunch that the headquarters in the United States could be more proactive by reaching out to the Asian offices before implementing initiatives without understanding the local cultural context. She expressed the disconnects they experienced, and made it clear that things that worked easily in the United States would not always work the same way in Asia.

Clearly, there are many improvements to be made within our global organizational structures to promote a more culturally sensitive way of working together across borders and reporting lines. But right now, there's a shortage of people equipped to navigate these different cultural markets and to act as effective liaisons between the United States and their global teams. If you're someone who is conscious of difference and makes an effort to develop your cultural fluency, you'll be in a stronger position to enter the global market successfully.

Global Opportunities Have Their Own Challenges

As in the United States, global leadership posts in Asia hinge on exposure to those opportunities, but also on having the skill set required to execute the work effectively. Many global companies don't do the best job of moving talent around, and selection is spotty at best; they lack the internal processes to build the necessary interaction skills in local Asian talent.

One senior partner at a private equity firm revealed: "There once was a time when the only way you could make it to senior management as an Asian American professional in the US was to do a stint in Asia." When I first started working in banking, the only managing director of Asian descent I could point to was based in Asia. Out of all the Asian Americans working in the firm, the only managing director was based in Hong Kong? Fortunately, that's not the case anymore, but as mentioned, the number of Asians who move to senior executive levels abroad isn't always high. Of course, just because a person is Asian American or might have ties to Asia doesn't mean they are immediately suited to working globally, so it's important that companies don't assume where their career path should be headed, either.

Moreover, Asian Americans who move to Asia to work can be viewed or treated as outsiders who need to do the work of understanding how to engage thoughtfully with the local business environment. Anyone would have to learn to treat the local teams with the right know-how—in other words, to be a culturally fluent leader.

Bridging Perceptions vs. Reality in Global Teams

Marie Segura, a consultant of Filipino, French, and Spanish heritage based in Manila, Philippines, reflects on the cultural dynamics that occur when local Filipinos start working with Asian Americans. Due to the rapid growth of industries in the Philippines, there has been a tremendous increase of workers from there in the global marketplace.

Marie reminded me that the local team members are not automatically going to respect you just because you look like them—you need to build credibility with them and show that you care about them personally. If you don't, given the strong collectivist orientation of the Filipino locals, they may resist or even unite against your leadership approach.

She shared that you can't expect a Filipino American to understand these nuances just because they look like other Filipinos. Marie states: "If the Filipino leader who grew up in the West [in the United States or the UK] leads with a cavalier attitude and assumes without a second thought that they're going to be readily accepted by their local team, they won't make it. If you don't put in the effort to get it right, it will be an uphill battle." Marie has seen many Filipino Americans attempt to lead in the Philippines and struggle when they don't demonstrate sincere care for their people. Neglecting to invest the time to build trust in these relationships and practice cultural fluency with their teams will immediately mark such leaders as outsiders.

There is tremendous opportunity in the global market, and if you're willing to do the hard work of bridging cultural values, the possibilities are limitless. But without investing in these relationships, you run the risk of alienating the cultures you're trying to engage.

If you are working outside of your home country for the first time, you may find that your cultural experience will be viewed through the dominant culture lens of your new environment. There is much evidence, as you see in the case of Australia, that the bamboo ceiling and "othering" exist in other cultures as well.

The opposite is true, too, with local Asian leaders often finding it difficult to move beyond their borders outside Asia. One Chinese leader I interviewed during a Conference Board study a few years ago said, "I don't think the senior leadership team could ever see someone from Asia come out to join the leadership team in Silicon Valley. We have the skills and mentality to succeed and drive tremendous growth, and we're making that happen right now, in our own country. But do they see us sitting with them in the power seats? Do they see us as fit to lead at that level? What will it take?"

The Bamboo Ceiling: Not Just an American Issue

The Leading for Change report from the Australian Human Rights Commission in 2018 found that only 3.3 percent of Australians of Asian heritage make it to senior executive levels, a stark contrast to the 95 percent of people with European backgrounds in those roles. Asian Australians make up about 12 percent of the Australian population. An earlier report from the Diversity Council in Australia found that there were significant barriers that were "locking out" Asian talent within Australian organizations: cultural bias and stereotyping, Western models that value self-promotion, lack of mentors, and cultural diversity not being utilized to its fullest potential. The traits of deference and respect for authority tended to be undervalued. Ming Long, the Malaysian Australian former CEO of Investa Property Group in Australia, shared in an interview for Yahoo Finance: "You think about leadership in Australia—it is a very white Anglo man. Six foot two, maybe they play rugby. I fit none of those things." She says Asian employees, especially if they're also women, are expected to be quiet, unthreatening, and good at math-oriented roles. If they don't conform, they may be labeled as aggressive. In a meeting with other executives where you are clearly the odd person out, the chance of stereotyping creeps in.

I've seen from my consulting work that Fortune 500 companies have a long way to go to build cultural fluency in how they run their business models, work with customers, and manage their diverse talent. Since it may take a while for companies to change, in place of that, equipping leaders to be adaptive in their thinking and doing, and to be attuned to the "heart" aspects of their business, will move the ball forward in engaging across differences. We need to be innovative about how we source, attract, and develop talent not only from a cultural perspective but from an array of competencies and job functions. How can you utilize your people among different locations in order for them to practice working in cultural contexts outside of their comfort zones?

CLOSER READ: As you review Anand's leadership story below, what resonates with you? Underline the skills he has used that you'd like to see practiced in your own workplace. Have you already practiced these skills? Could any of them be a growth area for you?

How Early Experiences Became an Asset for Leading on the Global Stage

Two things Anand Chokkalingam (first mentioned in chapter 9) learned from all the years he spent going to family meals and attending weekend events with his extended Tamil family in Northern California were respect for elders and the critical value of strong relationships. "The idea of respect, coming in with your head bowed (even if it's not literal). . . . The idea is 'I respect you . . . you have a position, or you're an elder and I respect your experience.' That was implicit in our family growing up."

His company, Gilead, was expanding its footprint in Japan, and Anand started doing some work with the new Japanese office while staying in the United States. "An aspect of Japanese culture is a sense of deference. What I understood more than many of my colleagues was: the absence of 'no' doesn't mean it's *not* no."

"If they're dancing around something and you're not getting a clear answer, you need to coax it out or get some more information; ease out the issues that are troubling them." This required an understanding of indirect communication styles and showing respect—something Anand had seen growing up—and showing it in a way that proved that he cared for his Japanese colleagues and their approaches. "It was a lot of high-touch conversations and time I needed to invest with them. I was willing to stay up late to speak with them, to reassure them or provide information that could clear up confusion. They appreciated this gesture, because most of the time, they were staying up late to accommodate *my* time zone because I was representing the headquarters' office."

"Our local Japan office knew their responsibility and was aware of the strict regulatory requirements there—so understanding their perspectives was essential. It took some time to figure out, and it didn't always go well. We really had to work at the relationship," Anand says. "I remember them saying to me, 'You know we are looking for help.' They were really saying, 'We need your help to succeed over here in Japan.'"

Anand responded with: "'I intend to help you succeed over there.' They were putting out a hand to ask for my help, and I had to be there for them. They needed to hear that and I needed to say, 'I'm committed to working with you, to serving you.'"

Anand traveled to Japan during this time, but most of the interactions happened by phone, which made it even more challenging when he was dealing with a high-context cultural environment.

"I learned that it's not just about executing on deliverables. You really have to show that you are there to help them, and you have to say it. [In the United States], we don't feel the need to say, 'We're on the same team.' But with global teams, saying those words is needed to build the relationship trust."

Later, Anand was working on a project with a global consortium of companies, comprising Gilead and a group of competitors. "At one point in our discussions, there was a concept that was being tossed around, but it was not going anywhere. So, I said, 'We still have to work out this detail, but let's remember that we already have XYZ covered and the pieces we need are ready . . . and in order to move forward, and we just need D to be resolved, as it's the only one in flux.'"

Because Anand had already worked on building up the trust in their relationships, that was all the team needed to hear to progress the project. "It wasn't rocket science, but someone had to say what was needed." Anand learned that stating the obvious was sometimes really important. "In that moment, I also learned that leading is not only about making decisions day to day, it's about who we are and how we bring our values to life in everyday encounters."

Navigating a Multicultural Workplace

Remember Mino Tsumura from chapter 4, the Japanese American whose Japanese colleagues considered him an outsider? You learned about how Mino's experience working with a global team did not go as smoothly as he initially thought it would. After getting over feeling disconnected with the culture, Mino had to learn viscerally that it was more than his fluency in the language or looking like his coworkers. He needed to become more curious about the invisible aspects of cultural difference and recognize when there was potential for conflict. Instead of reacting as he would with his American team, he responded by showing his colleagues that he was willing to work with their approaches. He saw how they opened up more to him in informal settings, when they socialized after hours. At the same time, he was deciphering what he could and could not change in his evolving leadership behaviors.

Today, Mino continues to navigate cultural issues as he manages teams across Asia. The group orientation (though it shows up differently than in Japan) is still present, manifesting in conference calls, decision-making points, and in-person meetings. But because of the skills he practiced in Japan, Mino is careful not to ignore these dynamics when they show up. He is more attuned to the power dynamics in the room for women, and notices when they may be less likely to share their opinions in the face of senior male colleagues in a meeting. He advocates for their voices to be heard and has refined the skill of asking questions and meeting them one-on-one to create a safe environment where they can contribute.

For Mino, being thrust into a different national culture helped him understand how his own cultural upbringing shaped his understanding of the world, and this became the catalyst that drove him to refine his intercultural leadership skills.

Making the Most of Global Opportunities

Throughout this book, you've learned ideas, tools, and concepts that are designed to help you lead effectively. But if everything that you've experienced to date in your workplace has occurred within the paradigm of US or Western corporate environments, how might that change or stay the same if you were working in Asia and on the broader global stage?

Putting It Together: A Three-Part Reflection

For Your Team or Organization

Identify, at the team or organizational level, opportunities for working more effectively in a global business landscape. What areas do you need to look at and improve?

☐ How we resolve disagreements virtually

☐ Team building in and outside of meetings

☐ The way we hand off work processes from office to office

☐ Onboarding new employees in a different region that we haven't met in person

For You Individually

Consider the following questions and pick one or two to respond to directly:

- What is your marketability on a global scale in your organization? Are you thinking about your career in a global capacity? Which geographical areas might need your expertise?

- How might a short-term or long-term global assignment expand your influence and network? What opportunities could position you well for future growth?

- How could you frame this interest in your development conversations with leadership as you consider next steps?

- If you were offered a position in a different region, how might you respond? How might you best prepare yourself for such an opportunity?

- If you work for a global organization, could you facilitate a talent exchange with another country location that could be win-win for both country locations? For example, could you have someone from a different region work with you for a year, and send someone from your country to another region?

For Your Personal Vision and Leadership Model

Refer back to the leadership model and goals you defined in chapter 6. As you answer these questions, think about how you might approach presenting your model to others with the global backdrop in mind.

- Are there cultural strengths you have not fully utilized that might be an asset for being a leader outside the United States, or within the United States but in a global oversight role?

- If your company's locations are based in the United States, are they taking a multicultural, global thinking approach to their future products and services? To the diverse communities they sell and market to?

- If a global role is in your future, what impact does this have on the networks you need to build in the upcoming year and the next steps in your personal life?

Working on a global scale and deeply understanding how different cultures approach their organization can be daunting. But I believe that if you can navigate this terrain, you'll be well positioned to add great value to the global business stage and ultimately contribute in positive ways to society. It's by doing the rich work of looking inward and reflecting on yourself as a leader that you'll be equipped to listen, learn, and meet people where they are. Developing the skill of cultural fluency can greatly enhance your work and personal interactions. Remember, differences are not always obvious. If you approach others in your work and your community with an open mind and heart as well as a growth mindset, the possibilities are endless.

Key Learning Points

- Global operations and processes are managed by people from different cultural perspectives. Leading successfully in this environment requires leaders who are culturally fluent and willing to effectively manage differences, not ignore them.

- Working in other regions and implementing strategies may mean acquiring intercultural skills that cross multiple boundaries and perspectives.

- Your skill set in terms of understanding different cultural communication styles and your commitment to being culturally fluent are perfectly aligned with the opportunities in today's global market. Global companies require leaders like you.

- By doing the work in this book, you're putting yourself in a stronger position to handle the challenges of leading authentically across cultures. There are tremendous opportunities for working in a global market where your skill set can be utilized.

12

WHAT KEEPS US GOING:
A CALL TO ACTION

*I don't know what I'm going to do next, but I feel
I have a responsibility to do something good.*

—KE HUY QUAN, Academy Award–winning actor,
Everything, Everywhere All at Once

How Far You've Come

When I caught up with Grace Chiang Nicolette, vice president of Programming and External Relations at the Center for Effective Philanthropy (CEP) last month, I enjoyed hearing her story about how increasing her cultural self-awareness helped her show agility in her leadership, in both managing up and managing her team. After working in investment banking in the United States, Grace spent seven years in China, first doing business development for a local technology company before completing a stint advising local philanthropies. She joined CEP upon her return to the United States and took on the challenge of examining how her experiences influenced her leadership. Throughout the lockdown, in the midst of uncertainty, her intentional leaning in to the diverse experiences of her team required that she meet team members where they were.

Even now, Grace is closely attuned to others' preferences and differences, while still being true to who she is at her core. For Grace, moving from a Minimization mindset to Adaptation meant regrounding in her identity, which included affirming the strength she derived from her faith and cultural identity and naming how those values impact her leadership. She puts this adaptive mindset to use multiple times throughout the workday, from working effectively with her CEO (how does he need to see or hear information?) to how she mobilizes her team members (how do I engage them and meet them where they are?)—as each brings different styles, cultural value preferences, and perceptions of her leadership. For Grace, practicing cultural fluency has become a continuous mindset.

Grace's story is one that I want all of you to experience: unpacking your past experiences, understanding difference, and leading from a place of authenticity. But it's not always easy to do this, and just because you're doing the hard work of understanding your cultural mindset doesn't mean everyone else is.

A few months ago, I debriefed an Asian American C-level leader on his cultural assessment. He had reached a strong level of cultural fluency, and while he was happy that he had acquired the skill of shifting his mindset and adapting his behaviors when working in diverse communities, he talked about the challenge of being in the Adaptation mindset when the majority of his organization was not. He saw things that others could not; he understood the way his mindset influenced the very questions that he asked, and those questions helped him arrive at more effective solutions for the company's new growth markets. He was seeing four or five alternative solutions and market paths where they saw only one—the one they were familiar with from the past twenty years. As he and I spoke about this, I realized that for him, going from point A to point D was automatic; he didn't even think about it.

Maybe you can relate to this story and share the frustration this leader felt. Not everyone lives in your brain, however, and not everyone has the same mindset toward difference that you do. You might not feel the need to communicate about *why* you're doing something, but everyone else can't necessarily see how you got from A to D—they need you to spell out B and C as well. This is why sharing your leadership model is so important; you have to work with those around you while still getting to an authentic place of leadership for yourself.

Having the tools to reset your cultural mindset, speaking up and breaking through when you and your team need to be impactful, and surrounding yourself with advocates who will support you in your development is critical. Having those skills and sharing them with others is the foundation for how you drive change and achieve results for both yourself and your organization.

What Are You Doing This For?

Identifying a meaningful vision and a stated purpose is crucial to this entire process; you will not change anything and people won't want to follow you if you can't give that to them. As I shared in part II, the hardest part of this work might be to name what's most important for you and to identify your vision. This should be compelling enough for you to embark on the challenge of leading effectively in a multicultural workplace. Can you name that vision and its associated goals? What challenges do you have where navigating cultural differences is necessary and critical to your success?

After reading this book, you have a few more tools and cultural approaches at your disposal. A more multicultural and adaptive leadership mindset takes intentional effort and ongoing practice. That means you need to ground yourself in your own cultural identity and find strength from it instead of running from it, and better know how to draw upon that strength so that you can use it intentionally when working in diverse spaces. It also means you have leaned into the uniqueness that you bring, especially if you've been socialized to fit in and "go with the program."

Being authentic and being culturally adaptive may seem contradictory, but they are actually two sides of the same coin. Being culturally fluent doesn't mean that you have to lose your authenticity in the process. You can adapt to different people without losing sight of your core values, which is why it is important to define what those are.

Each of the leaders in this book had to reconcile who they were with what others expected them to be. That also meant being adaptive, because others expected them to operate in one mode, even when they felt something else on the inside. But after working on it and applying these techniques, they have all gotten closer to discovering their genuine leadership voice. This didn't happen overnight; they encountered difficulties and went through a series of learnings to arrive at their current growth state. They recovered from mishaps and got back up to try again. They did this multiple times. If you've been through my firm's leadership cohort programs, you're familiar with this approach. If not, this is the work you've done throughout this book: to start the process of discovering your unique self and applying that to how you lead.

Look how far you've come already. You've designed your own leadership model and explored your cultural identity and values and how they've shaped you. You've assessed your cultural fluency, taken a deeper look at your life experiences, started to try on some new skills in new areas, and had courageous conversations with important stakeholders in your life about the goals you care about. You're now ready to share your model with others and begin putting it into practice. All of this means that you're another step closer to practicing this new leadership in a more authentic way than you were yesterday. Having done this work myself multiple times, I can't guarantee that every step will be easy, but I can promise you that it'll be worth it.

Harnessing Your Life Journey as Fuel to Help Asian American Youth

Since 2010, Preeti Sriratana has served as the board chair for Apex for Youth, an organization that helps empower underserved Asian and immigrant kids from preK to post–high school. In his own words, Preeti seeks to "open more doors for others and create systems that put others in a better position to do good for society." His philosophy and dedication to diversity informs both his firm's architectural work as well as his work with Apex.

Preeti's parents emigrated from Thailand to Chicago, where Preeti was born. When he was two, his family moved to rural central Illinois. Preeti's childhood and youth were filled with painful moments of feeling like an outsider. As he recalls: "I was bullied at school all the time while my parents were working eighty-hour weeks. I was not a good student, not good at math like I was 'supposed' to be." In the nineties, there was a lot of hostility toward Asians. His home was frequently vandalized with racial slurs graffitied on the walls. The family would find garbage tossed out in front of the house on a regular basis. "Every morning I opened the door, I'd be nervous about what I would find outside. If someone threw out their garbage in front of our house, I'd clean it up before I went to school. I was afraid that people in our neighborhood could see it."

Preeti wasn't mentally or academically prepared for college and got kicked out after his first semester. Eventually, however, he graduated from the University of Illinois with a degree in architecture. Being accepted into Columbia's graduate program in architecture took Preeti to New York City. He remembers, "I got there only because of all the kind people who mentored me, and I wanted to pay it forward and get involved with an organization that invested in youth like me." He started volunteering for Apex for Youth, where he later became the board chair. He was later accepted into Harvard Kennedy School for Public Policy with an application essay about how he could become stronger in this role with this youth organization.

"Apex was founded in 1992 and it was a very grassroots organization when I joined. They were actually looking to close, but we didn't, and we grew it through the recession of 2008. When I first became the chair, Apex had a budget of 150K and there was one full-time staff person serving eighty kids. After rebuilding 75 percent of the board and growing our infrastructure, it is now a $6 million organization serving 2,500 youth from preK to post–high school. We have fifty staff, including social work-ers." Apex introduced remote programs during the pandemic and has reached youth in more than twenty states. "The families of these kids don't have the resources to do it for themselves, so they have no idea how to do it for their children. We filled the gap."

It's not just in his volunteer work that Preeti strives to make a differ-ence. When he and his two cofounders launched the architecture firm Modellus Novus (MN), they sought to change the face of architecture and centered their firm on the values of diversity and inclusion. Designing spaces for "the many" is the firm's rallying cry, and they live their values by having an exceptionally diverse firm with strong retention rates. MN is made up of 50 percent people of color and 50 percent women, which is uncharacteristic of the architecture industry. MN renovated David Geffen Hall (Lincoln Center) and designed the restaurant Tatiana, recognized by Pete Wells of the *New York Times* as the #1 restaurant of 2023—no small feat for a New York City restaurant.

"When I inherited Apex and when I cofounded Modellus Novus, it was critical that I worked with people whose values aligned with mine. There is no compromising on values." Preeti believes that leadership is what one exercises and thus is a verb, not just a title or a noun.

Preeti holds no pretense about the challenges he encountered grow-ing up, and knows that they fueled his desire to help kids who remind him of his experience. His childhood touchstone was his grandmother, who helped raise him. A warm, loving, and incredibly encouraging person, she gave him a sense of security when he came home from a school where he had no friends. On her watch, Preeti grew up making models and building a lot of forts at home, which may have been an early indication of his interest in architecture. He remembers his grandmother with fondness: "When I was sixteen, she passed away suddenly from a stroke. The feeling I had in that moment has been the motivation and fuel for everything that I do."

Throughout this book, you've also delved deeper into your Asian American experience and how it has shaped you. We are all part of this larger community, and honing your capacity to lead effectively goes hand in hand with helping others find a voice and giving back. Once you've put your own leadership model into place, it's time to start thinking about how you might help others who are coming up through the ranks. Whether it's in the form of mentoring younger Asian Americans in your industry, volunteering in an organization that needs your voice and expertise, or advocating for your employee resource group at your company, it's important to consider how you're going to "pay it forward."

Why This Matters: The Future of Asian American Voices

One marketing leader at a large retail company shared with me after a keynote: "I've learned that language [Spanish] is the heart tie that connects the Latino community together, with all their diversity of backgrounds. But with the Asian American customers, they are still an enigma! How do I even begin to put my arm around this demographic?"

Creating an Authentic Brand: Sanzo and 1587 Sneakers

Sanzo is a brand that was the brainchild of Filipino American Sandro Roco. Born in Queens and raised in New Jersey, Sandro sought to create a low-calorie drink as an alternative to sugary sodas. His line of seltzers uses flavors like lychee, calamansi, and yuzu—familiar fruits in Southeast Asia and East Asia. Instead of limiting his product to Asian supermarkets and specialty shops, he seeks to market it to a broader audience as part of his mission to increase Asian American representation in grocery stores across the country.

Sandro was new to the industry when his idea started to germinate in 2018. At the time, he was living in New York City and had started to appreciate his Asian American identity and lean into it more fully. He became inspired by the growth of Asian-inspired creative goods and restaurants in the city. In embracing his heritage and trying to share it with the world, Sandro has created a unique product that's gaining momentum. I recently saw Sanzo seltzers on my last trip to Target as well as at my corner grocery store in New York. When I picked up a six-pack of the drinks from my local grocery store, the cans featured photos of Jeremy Lin—the basketball player who enthralled the Asian American community when he led the New York Knicks to a memorable seven-game winning streak in 2012.

Sneaker brand 1587 also intentionally integrates the Asian American cultural experience. Launched by Asian Americans Adam King and Sam Hyun, 1587 is marketed toward the Asian American community. Its name references the year the first Asians—Filipino sailors—set foot on North American soil. Some of the sneaker styles contain humorous messages like "Leave your shoes at the door," which refers to the practice of Asians requiring guests to remove their shoes before entering the house. Total sneaker sales in 2023 hit $23 billion—and sales are expected to grow at a rate of 4.6 percent through 2028. Adam and Sam have embraced their unique multicultural perspective and created something to appeal to Asian Americans and a broader market.

As you can see from these two examples, there is room in the marketplace to lean into your authentic cultural self while creating innovative products for the broader marketplace.

The longer I work within and for the Asian American community, the more I'm struck by the sheer diversity of this growing population: Asian Americans have the widest income disparity and are heterogeneous in terms of ethnicity, variations of identity, language and dialects, socioeconomic and religious backgrounds, and how they choose to live their lives. In that messy complexity lies the hidden potential of what they can offer their employers and communities. This diversity is largely unknown to others, and Asian Americans are in the best position to articulate their challenges and opportunities so that they are no longer lumped into one big monolith. They are the ones who can define who they want to be and not be labeled with some random characteristics of one or two Asian "types" that fall short of who they really are.

As Asian Americans explore the similarities of their family experiences and tease out the myriad of differences that they embody in their origin and immigration stories, their array of insights and unique perspectives can open the door to innovation for their companies, communities, and schools. Whether you came here recently for graduate studies and still are perplexed by the challenge of navigating the US-centric corporate structure, or your family has been here for multiple generations and you are now just making sense of your evolving identity, or you're experiencing a dozen more scenarios I could name—you bring a valuable perspective, a point of view that only you can contribute.

Moving to a Place of Thriving

My hope for you is that you go beyond survival to a place of thriving. I want you to have a fresh paradigm for what wakes you up in the morning. That's why I've been focusing so much on digging deep and homing in on the internal aspects of your leadership. Now that you know your "why," I can't wait to hear how you put into daily action leadership behaviors that are authentic to you.

I wrote this book to help Asians individually carve out their own idea of success, whether that's professional or personal. That means finding language and approaches that work for you, to motivate yourself and others to action. Applying the leadership skills I talk about here doesn't necessarily mean that you need to aspire to be the CEO of a company; that's not the end goal for many people. But I want you to be a few steps closer to knowing yourself better, defining how you'd like to engage with others in a multicultural workplace, and expressing your leadership behaviors in a way that feels natural for you.

When I wrote *Breaking the Bamboo Ceiling*, we had just adopted our son from South Korea. Last week (as I write this), I dropped him off at college where he's interested in pursuing film. My initial reaction to his desire to study film was to think: *Are you sure you want to do that?* I know so little about the industry, and as I anticipate the obstacles and the potential discrimination he might face in the entertainment field in front of and behind the camera, I worry. But I also want to do whatever I can to support him in his dream and to help him realize that he can be anything. The reason I continue to do this work is so that young people like my son can choose their careers without having to face barriers and stereotypes because of the way they look. I want our young people to pursue their true callings without having to trade off too much of their personal authenticity.

As I hugged my son goodbye in his dorm room, I told him that we would be here whenever he needed it. I wished for him, as I wish for the readers of this book: "May you fulfill your potential, know when and how to adapt to others, and still stay true to yourself."

Summary Themes for Reflection

- Culture is the "software of the mind" that influences every human interaction, showing up in visible and invisible ways.

- It's vital to **obtain an accurate snapshot** of how you respond to and make sense of differences. Understanding how you think about difference can inform a successful strategy that allows you to engage interculturally.

- Be aware of where you are on your career journey, and where you're headed. As you review the three phases—producer, credibility builder, and organizational influencer—consider: Are you starting to enter a new phase or on the cusp of doing so? And remember that career advancement is not always linear.

- Your cultural values have shaped you in distinctive and significant ways; that's why examining how your early life experiences have influenced you is critical to growing in your leadership skills.

- With this in mind, **be intentional** about where you want to go. Clarify your vision and your goals for learning. Then, identify the skills you need to develop to get there.

- Be aware that you will encounter bias from others. The model minority myth and the perpetual foreigner syndrome are realities that you will continue to face in the workplace.

- Keep in mind that it's just as crucial to **build relationships** up, down, and across the organization and engage with your ERGs as it is to perform your job responsibilities.

- **Build resilience** by learning to recover quickly. Surround yourself with a diverse array of people who can support you as you get up and try again. Commit to building a community of trusted colleagues who will give you honest feedback when you need it.

- What makes this learning possible and makes it stick is having a growth mindset that allows you to believe that your skills and talents can be developed—a key component to becoming a culturally fluent leader. Leading with a learning mindset and an attitude of curiosity will serve you well.

- A core part of this learning is to **find your authentic voice** as a leader who connects in meaningful ways with people who are not like you. This unique voice will be indispensable as you make a difference on the global stage.

- Make your well-being and mental health a priority. **Practice reframing** disempowering inner voices that increase isolation, and reframe them with empowering beliefs.

- Learn to **leverage your cultural perspective** and draw upon its strengths. You can't change your organization on your own, but you can be a new—and powerful—voice for change.

- Finally, **pay it forward** to a younger person. There is always someone who is less experienced (e.g., a college student or a new hire) who can benefit from your wisdom.

APPENDIX

PROFESSIONAL ASSOCIATIONS AND COMMUNITY GROUPS

Looking for additional inspiration, support, and networking? A place to volunteer your expertise and get more involved in the Asian community? This appendix lists professional and student organizations that you might be interested in checking out further.

Professional Associations and Community Groups

We have used the descriptions of these organizations from their websites. I encourage you to review each organization's website or contact the offices directly. Kudos to Mathea Li Olson for her work on this! If you'd like to see other organizations listed in a future edition, please let us know at *info@ hyunassociates.com.*

Note that listing here does not imply official endorsement by the author or publisher of this book.

AAPI CIVIC ENGAGEMENT FUND
(*https://aapifund.org/*)

AAPI Civic Engagement Fund's belief that Asian Americans and Pacific Islanders are integral to strengthening America's multiracial democracy and transforming systemic conditions to improve the quality of life for all is supported through grant-making, movement capacity (training), and research.

ACE NEXTGEN
(*https://www.acenextgen.org/*)

ACE NextGen is the millennial arm of the National ACE (Asian/Pacific Islander American Chamber of Commerce and Entrepreneurship); its aim is to build a dynamic community of AAPI entrepreneurs, fostering continuous growth and an entrepreneurial mindset. It offers resources and relationships for long-term community impact.

ALSO KNOWN AS
(AKA; *https://www.alsoknownas.org/*)

Founded in 1996, AKA focuses on empowering the voices of adult international adoptees, while providing resources and space to acknowledge the loss of birth country, culture, language, and biological family. It provides networking opportunities for adult adoptees, mentoring programs for children and teens, and educational workshops for parents.

APEX FOR YOUTH
(*https://apexforyouth.org/*)

Apex for Youth empowers underserved Asian and immigrant youth from low-income families in New York City. Launched in 1992 by five friends with a shoestring budget of $2,000, Apex offer programs for grades K–12, including two virtual programs for students anywhere in the United States. It also sponsors reading programs, afterschool programs, athletics, mental health education, and a mentoring program that has recently seen 100 percent of its twelfth graders go to college.

APIA SCHOLARS
(https://apiascholars.org/)

APIA Scholars provides scholarships, with a focus on students at or below the poverty level who trace their heritage to countries, territories, or lands in Asia or the Pacific Islands. APIA Scholars offers holistic college-to-career programs, scholarships, higher education research and policy, and partnerships. It has launched a mental health initiative for college students to build awareness of the impacts of mental health challenges within the APIA community.

ASCEND LEADERSHIP
(https://www.ascendleadership.org/)

Ascend is a global network of Pan-Asian professionals; its mission is to build community and ignite change by developing, elevating, and empowering the API leaders of tomorrow. It collaborates with nineteen professional chapters and more than forty-five student chapters to offer national and local chapter events to cultivate leaders who drive positive transformation within workplaces.

ASIA SOCIETY
(https://asiasociety.org/)

Established in 1956, the Asia Society aims to foster a harmonious global future by promoting dialogue, collaboration, and diverse insights across policy, arts, education, and other sectors. Through partnerships and by embracing various perspectives, it seeks innovative solutions for challenges, aiming toward a sustainable and prosperous world. A nonpartisan nonprofit organization, it is focused on three pillars: Arts and Culture, Education, and Policy.

ASIAN AMERICAN BAR ASSOCIATION OF NEW YORK
(AABANY; *https://www.aabany.org/)*

AABANY's mission is to foster the meaningful participation of Asian American Pacific Islanders in the legal field through the study, practice, and fair administration of law. It advances diversity and inclusion through professional development, legal scholarship, advocacy, and engagement of the AAPI community.

ASIAN AMERICAN FEDERATION
(AAF; *https://www.aafederation.org/*)

AAF seeks to raise the influence and well-being of the pan–Asian American community through research, policy advocacy, public awareness, and organizational development. It addresses immigration, mental health, and civic engagement. Collaborating with government officials and private backers, AAF publishes research reports and offers small-business programs, furnishing resources like legal aid, financial support, translation services, and lease assistance for the Asian American community.

THE ASIAN AMERICAN FOUNDATION
(TAAF; *https://www.taaf.org/*)

TAAF serves the Asian American and Pacific Islander community in their pursuit of belonging and prosperity that is free from discrimination, slander, and violence. Founded in 2021 in response to the rise in anti-Asian hate and to address the long-standing underinvestment in AAPI communities, TAAF funds best-in-class organizations working to mobilize against hate and violence, educate communities, and reclaim Asian narratives through its core pillars of Anti-Hate, Education, Narrative Change, and Resources and Representation.

ASIAN AMERICAN JOURNALISTS ASSOCIATION
(AAJA; *https://www.aaja.org/*)

AAJA is a national nonprofit membership organization that advocates on behalf of AAPIs in the newsroom on the front lines for stronger representation and more inclusion. AAJA has advocated for diversity in media and unbiased representation of communities of color. With over 1,500 members spanning the United States and Asia, AAJA promotes AAPI journalists' presence in leadership roles, fostering accurate coverage of AAPI communities and engaging young individuals in journalism.

ASIAN AMERICAN LEGAL DEFENSE AND EDUCATION FUND
(AALDEF; *https://www.aaldef.org/*)

The AALDEF was founded in 1974 by Margaret Fung to promote and protect the civil rights of Asian Americans. Today, it is a national organization working with Asian American communities across the United States to secure human rights by combining litigation, advocacy, and education.

ASIAN AMERICANS ADVANCING JUSTICE
(AAJC; *https://www.advancingjustice-aajc.org/*)

AAJC is an affiliation of five organizations whose mission is to advance civil and human rights for Asian Americans and to build and promote a fair and equitable society for all. Some of its programs include Census, Anti-Asian Hate, Media Diversity, Whole Story Education Campaign, Immigrant Rights, Voting Rights, Telecommunications and Technology, and Racial Justice.

ASIAN AMERICANS FOR EQUALITY
(AAFE; *https://www.aafe.org/*)

AAFE is dedicated to advancing racial, social, and economic justice by fostering community development, affordable housing, economic opportunities, and multilingual services in New York. Established in 1974, AAFE has grown into an organization rooted in immigrant neighborhoods, advocating for underserved communities through initiatives like housing development, small-business support, community services, and youth engagement.

ASIAN AMERICANS WITH DISABILITIES INITIATIVE
(AADI; *https://www.aadinitiative.org/*)

The AADI is a nonprofit organization founded in July 2021 to provide accessible resources to empower the next generation of disabled Asian American leaders to confront anti-Asian racism and ableism within their communities. AADI has always been youth-driven and grounded in the spirit of intersectionality.

ASIAN AMERICAN WRITERS' WORKSHOP, INC. (AAWW; *https://aaww.org/*)

The AAWW is a national nonprofit organization dedicated to publishing, incubating, and amplifying Asian and Asian diasporic storytelling and artistry. Since its founding in 1991, it has worked to create a unique literary space that operates at the intersection of art and social justice.

ASIAN AND PACIFIC ISLANDER AMERICAN HEALTH FORUM (APIAHF; *https://www.apiahf.org/*)

APIAHF is the oldest and largest health advocacy organization committed to enhancing the well-being of Asian Americans and Native Hawaiians/Pacific Islanders (AA and NH/PI). With offices in San Francisco and Washington, DC, APIAHF influences policy, mobilizes communities, and strengthens programs and organizations to improve the health of Asian Americans, Native Hawaiians, and Pacific Islanders.

ASIAN AND PACIFIC ISLANDERS FOR LGBT EQUALITY–LOS ANGELES (*https://www.apiequalityla.org/*)

The mission of API Equality–LA is to empower Asian and Pacific Islander communities to foster LGBTQ, racial, and social justice. It focuses on issues such as mental health and community wellness, and offers youth programs to support Asian and other immigrant communities.

ASIAN AND PACIFIC ISLANDERS WITH DISABILITIES IN CALIFORNIA (*https://www.apidisabilities.org/*)

Giving a voice and face to Asians and Pacific Islanders with physical, mental, and developmental disabilities, Asian and Pacific Islanders with Disabilities in California breaks down barriers by providing information and education to the community, training young adults to become advocates, and connecting families to resources.

ASIAN HUSTLE NETWORK
(AHN; *https://www.asianhustlenetwork.com/*)

AHN is a global network of Asian entrepreneurs and creatives. Through its engaged community of 250,000 members around the world, its storytelling, and its programming, AHN seeks to create an ecosystem to inspire, uplift, and connect members to the people and resources who will take their pursuits to the next level.

ASIAN MENTAL HEALTH COLLECTIVE
(AMHC; *https://www.asianmhc.org/*)

AMHC aims to address the unique challenges faced by individuals of the Asian diaspora in the context of evolving personal well-being awareness. By integrating cultural values with modern mental health concepts, AMHC aspires to make mental health approachable, acceptable, and accessible to Asian communities worldwide by bridging generational and cultural gaps within families and helping individuals locate Asian therapists across the United States.

ASIAN PACIFIC ISLANDER QUEER WOMEN & TRANSGENDER COMMUNITY (APIQWTC)
(*https://apiqwtc.org/about-us/*)

APIQWTC provides opportunities for Asian Pacific Islander queer women and transgender people to socialize, network, build community, engage in intergenerational organizing, and increase community visibility.

ASIANS IN ADVERTISING
(*https://www.asiansinadvertising.com/*)

The mission of Asians in Advertising is to develop a free community, create opportunities, and help elevate Asians to higher leadership positions. It seeks to connect Asians in the advertising industry, elevate them to the next level, and showcase their talents. Its programs include the Future Asian Leaders scholarship and the Nextgen Mentorship program.

CENTER FOR ASIAN AMERICAN MEDIA
(CAAM; *https://caamedia.org/*)

A nonprofit organization dedicated to presenting stories that convey the richness and diversity of Asian American experiences to the broadest audience possible, CAAM funds, produces, exhibits, and distribute works in film, television, and digital media.

CENTER FOR ASIAN PACIFIC AMERICAN WOMEN
(CAPAW; *https://capaw.org/*)

CAPAW promotes leadership skills among Asian American, Native Hawaiian, and Pacific Islander women. It offers the APAWLI Fellowship Program, a leadership initiative that asks participants to embark on a community impact project. CAPAW holds regional conferences and an annual national leadership summit.

CHINA'S CHILDREN INTERNATIONAL
(CCI; *https://chinaschildreninternational.org/*)

Founded in 2011, CCI stands as a pioneering global network and community initiative created for and led by Chinese adoptees. In 2020, CCI formalized its status as a 501(c)(3) nonprofit organization in the United States, committed to empowering and uniting adult Chinese adoptees worldwide.

CHINESE-AMERICAN PLANNING COUNCIL
(CPC; *https://www.cpc-nyc.org/about-us*)

The CPC's mission is to promote the social and economic empowerment of Chinese American, immigrant, and low-income communities. CPC is the nation's largest Asian American social services organization and the trusted partner to sixty thousand individuals and families striving to achieve goals in their education, family, community, and career.

CHINESE ADOPTEE ALLIANCE
(CAA; *https://fccny.org/*)

CAA, previously known as FCCNY (Families with Children from China New York), emerged in the early 1990s as a parent support group situated in Manhattan. However, CAA has since transformed into an adoptee-centered entity, dedicating its efforts to cater to the broader Chinese adoptee community and the worldwide network of adoptees and their supporters.

COALITION OF ASIAN PACIFICS IN ENTERTAINMENT
(CAPE; *https://www.capeusa.org/*)

Founded in 1991, CAPE champions diversity by educating, connecting, and empowering Asian American and Pacific Islander artists and leaders in entertainment and media.

COMMITTEE OF 100
(*https://www.committee100.org/*)

The Committee of 100 is a nonpartisan organization of prominent Chinese Americans in business, government, academia, and the arts. Its stated purposes are to advocate for full participation of Chinese Americans in American society, to act as a public policy resource, and to advance constructive dialogue and relationships between the people and leaders of the United States and greater China.

COUNCIL OF KOREAN AMERICANS
(CKA; *https://councilka.org/*)

CKA's mission is to amplify the national voice of Korean American leaders and increase the influence of the Korean American community. It provides initiatives to strengthen the collaboration of Korean American leaders across sectors, celebrates Korean American identity and history, provides Emerging Leaders Scholarships to students who are interested in the Korean American community, and connects these students to the opportunity to participate in a public service internship program.

DISABILITY:IN
(*https://disabilityin.org/*)

Disability:IN is a nonprofit resource advocating for business disability inclusion worldwide. It sponsors educational programs for talent and companies, a library of instructional materials for empowering disability inclusion, and a current library of news related to business and the disability community.

FOUNDATION FOR FILIPINA WOMEN'S NETWORK
(FWN; *https://filipinawomensnetwork.org/*, *https://www.ffwn.org/*)

Founded in 2001, FWN is dedicated to supporting career-oriented women with Philippine heritage, empowering them to excel in both public and private sectors. FWN's 100 Most Influential Filipina Women Awardees program selects exceptional women from diverse sectors and countries who have left a significant impact on their professions and communities, aiming to showcase Filipina women as integral contributors to the global economy.

GOLD HOUSE
(*https://goldhouse.org/*)

Gold House is a referral-based, member-driven collective that unites and invests in Asian Pacific creators and companies. Members are successful Asian founders, leading creative voices in entertainment, and C-suite/partner-level executives.

HMONG AMERICAN PARTNERSHIP
(HAP; *https://hmong.org/*)

HAP is committed to empowering the community, celebrating the strengths of Hmong cultures, and unlocking their full potential. It achieves this mission through culturally sensitive social services that enhance the lives of individuals and families in its diverse communities. HAP focuses on strengthening neighborhoods by providing opportunities for housing, community, and economic development. It promotes the rich heritage of its ethnic communities, acknowledging and honoring their contributions.

HMONG NATIONAL DEVELOPMENT, INC.
(HND; *https://hndinc.org/*)

Founded in 1993, HND is the leading national advocacy group for Hmong Americans. For over two decades, HND has supported Hmong nonprofits, promoted relevant legislation, fostered youth leadership, and gained recognition for its Hmong National Development Conference.

IAMADOPTEE
(*https://iamadoptee.org/*)

IAMAdoptee was established by adoptees to build an online hub of mental health resources for intercountry-adopted individuals, guiding them through their experiences. Through shared stories and focused campaigns, IAMAdoptee supports adoptees in connecting and understanding the diverse effects of international adoption.

INTERCOUNTRY ADOPTEE VOICES
(ICAV; *https://intercountryadopteevoices.com/*)

ICAV connects intercountry adoptees around the world and offers them education and support. ICAV provides a secure platform for adoptees to shape their perspectives throughout their adoption journey and advocates for adoptee rights and the complexities of intercountry adoption.

JAPANESE AMERICAN CITIZENS LEAGUE
(JACL; *https://jacl.org/*)

Founded in 1929, JACL is the oldest and largest Asian American civil rights organization in the United States. JACL advocates for civil rights, combats injustice, and promotes cultural and educational values for Japanese Americans and others affected by discrimination.

JAPAN SOCIETY
(*https://japansociety.org/*)

Founded in 1907, Japan Society in New York has become a leading provider of top-tier Japanese-focused content for English speakers in North America. Through a wide range of programs, it offers access to information, cultural experiences, and constructive discussions on pertinent issues between the United States, Japan, and East Asia.

KOREAN AMERICAN ADOPTIVE FAMILY NETWORK
(KAAN; *https://www.wearekaan.org/***)**

Founded in 1998, KAAN is entirely run by volunteers and operates as a distinct initiative within the Foundation for Enhancing Communities, serving as its fiscal sponsor. Its primary objective is to enhance the well-being of Korean-born adoptees by fostering connections within the community and facilitating opportunities for meaningful conversations, education, and assistance.

KOREAN AMERICAN COMMUNITY FOUNDATION
(KACF; *https://kacfny.org/***)**

KACF provides grants and organizational development support to nonprofit groups working to address the most pressing needs in the Korean American community and beyond. KACF addresses housing and homelessness, mental health, unemployment, healthcare access, domestic violence, budget equity and advocacy, research, and narrative change.

KOREAN AMERICAN FAMILY SERVICE CENTER
(KAFSC; *https://www.kafsc.org/***)**

KAFSC was established in 1989 to support domestic violence and sexual assault victims in the Korean American community from a combined prevention and intervention perspective while remaining sensitive to their cultural setting. Their staff is 100 percent bilingual and bicultural. KAFSC provides counseling, education, and advocacy, and recently held its twenty-fifth annual Silent March Against Domestic Violence.

THE KOREA SOCIETY
(*https://www.koreasociety.org/***)**

The Korea Society is a nonprofit, nonpartisan organization with individual and corporate members. This organization is committed to enhancing awareness, comprehension, and collaboration between the United States and Korea, focusing exclusively on this mission.

NATIONAL ASIAN/PACIFIC ISLANDER AMERICAN CHAMBER OF COMMERCE AND ENTREPRENEURSHIP
(ACE; *https://www.nationalace.org/*)

National ACE is a dedicated advocate for the interests of Asian American and Pacific Islander (AAPI) businesses, aiming to create positive change and progress for AAPI entrepreneurs and leaders. Through various means such as issue promotion, economic development, community building, grants, and fostering new AAPI entrepreneurs, National ACE works to advance the goals and aspirations of the AAPI business community.

NATIONAL ASIAN PACIFIC AMERICAN BAR ASSOCIATION
(NAPABA; *https://www.napaba.org/*)

NAPABA offers multiple programs designed to increase the number of AAPI partners at major law firms and achieve optimal representation in every facet of the profession.

NATIONAL ASIAN PACIFIC AMERICAN WOMEN'S FORUM
(NAPAWF; *https://www.napawf.org/*)

NAPAWF was founded in 1996 and stands as the sole entity dedicated to empowering AAPI women and girls, enabling them to influence crucial decisions that impact their lives, families, and communities. Through a reproductive justice approach, it empowers AAPI women and girls to shape policies and instigate systemic transformation in the United States.

NATIONAL ASSOCIATION OF ASIAN AMERICAN PROFESSIONALS
(NAAAP; *https://www.naaap.org/*)

Founded in 1982, NAAAP is a professional organization for Asian and Asian American professionals and their allies in North America, with thirty chapters, several thousand active members, and a reach of more than twenty-seven thousand professionals. NAAAP provides members with resources for leadership development, networking, and community service opportunities and provides a platform to elevate Asian excellence. It partners closely with employee resource groups and holds annual national conventions hosted in various cities across the country.

NATIONAL COUNCIL OF ASIAN PACIFIC AMERICANS (NCAPA; *https://www.ncapaonline.org/*)

Established in 1996, NCAPA is a Washington, DC–based coalition of thirty-eight national Asian Pacific American organizations. NCPA aims to advocate for the interests of the larger Asian American and Native Hawaiian Pacific Islander communities, using collective strengths to shape policies and public narratives for equity and justice.

NATIONAL QUEER ASIAN PACIFIC ISLANDER ALLIANCE (NQAPIA; *https://www.nqapia.org/*)

Established in 2005, NQAPIA empowers LGBTQ+ Asians and Pacific Islanders by fostering movement capacity, advocating for policies, and providing representation. NQAPIA is deeply rooted in the enduring traditions of resistance, resilience, and community-building among LGBTQ+ Asians and Pacific Islanders, uniting dozens of small, volunteer-run groups nationwide.

OCA–ASIAN PACIFIC AMERICAN ADVOCATES (*https://www.ocanational.org/*)

Dedicated to social, political, and economic well-being of Asian Americans and Pacific Islanders, OCA–Asian Pacific American Advocates provides leadership training; internship programs in the Washington, DC, area; DEI workshops; and more.

PHILIPPINE NURSES ASSOCIATION OF AMERICA (PNAA; *https://mypnaa.org/*)

Established in 1979, PNAA is a nonprofit nursing organization with fifty-five chapters and over five thousand members. PNAA prioritizes the welfare of Filipino American nurses, offering mentorship, leadership programs, and conferences in the United States and Philippines and advocating for nursing policy and diversity.

THE PRISM FOUNDATION
(FORMERLY GAPA FOUNDATION; *https://theprismfoundation.org/*)

The Prism Foundation, located in the San Francisco Bay Area, focuses on addressing critical issues affecting the Asian and Pacific Islander LGBTQIA+ community while supporting innovative programs and individuals. Its efforts include providing academic scholarships to nontraditional API LGBTQIA+ students and offering core funding to underresourced local community organizations and projects, with an emphasis on nurturing their growth through mentorship and leadership development.

RIGHT TO BE
(FORMERLY HOLLABACK; *https://righttobe.org/*)

Right to Be trains individuals and organizations how to respond to, intervene in, and heal from harassment. Using real-life scenarios, it aims to equip participants with tools they can use to help themselves and others when they encounter a tough or dangerous situation. Right to Be offers training on topics of bystander intervention to address anti-Asian sentiment and informative webinars on topics like street harassment and antisemitic harassment.

SOCIETY OF ASIAN SCIENTISTS AND ENGINEERS
(SASE; *https://www.saseconnect.org/*)

SASE's mission is to empower Asian heritage scientists and engineers by facilitating their growth in education and professional opportunities, ensuring the realization of their full career potential. SASE is active at the collegiate and professional levels and offers scholarships to full-time students cosponsored by major organizations. It seeks to provide opportunities for members to make positive contributions to their local communities.

SOUTH ASIAN BAR ASSOCIATION
(SABA; *https://sabanorthamerica.com/*)

SABA is a national bar association dedicated to the needs, concerns, and interests of lawyers of South Asian heritage. With twenty-nine chapters throughout the United States and Canada, SABA hosts an annual conference and various programs for professional development. SABA is committed to promoting the professional development of the South Asian legal community through networking, advocacy, and pro bono opportunities.

SOUTH ASIAN TRAILBLAZERS
(https://www.southasiantrailblazers.com/)

South Asian Trailblazers is a media platform and community that elevates and convenes South Asian leaders through a podcast and publication. It deep-dives into the journeys of trailblazing South Asians and hosts various events, including live podcasts with trailblazers, intimate dinners, and networking mixers with South Asian professionals across industries.

SOUTHEAST ASIAN DEVELOPMENT CENTER
(https://seadcenter.org/)

The Southeast Asian Development Center, established as a nonprofit organization in 1977, is committed to elevating children, youth, and families from Cambodia, Laos, and Vietnam out of poverty. Their focus revolves around assisting low-income and vulnerable Southeast Asian Americans by addressing their basic needs and imparting critical skills essential for building successful futures.

STAND AGAINST HATRED
(https://www.standagainsthatred.org/)

Stand Against Hatred is an affiliate of Americans Advancing Justice where the public can document hate incidents. Though there is no direct reporting to law enforcement, this organization has provided a steady report of the number of hate incidents experienced by Asians in America for several years.

STOP AAPI HATE
(https://stopaapihate.org/)

Stop AAPI Hate is a national coalition fighting against racism and racial injustice targeting Asian Americans and Pacific Islanders. It works with local communities and government stakeholders to document the rise of anti-AAPI hate and dismantle the systems that allow it to persist.

TAIWANESE AMERICAN CITIZENS LEAGUE
(TACL; *https://tacl.org/*)

Established in 1985, TACL is dedicated to enhancing the well-being of Taiwanese Americans in the United States through its mission of fostering leadership, identity, networking, and citizenship. Operating under the TACL umbrella, Taiwanese American Professionals (TAP) chapters form a nationwide network of young professionals, while TACL's programs encompass all ages and emphasize youth leadership and identity development.

WOMANKIND
(*https://www.iamwomankind.org/*)

Womankind uses the multidimensionality of its Asian heritage to work alongside survivors of gender-based violence as they build a path to healing. The group was founded in 1982 (and formerly known as NY Asian Women's Center), and its inception came merely six years after the inauguration of the city's first domestic violence shelter.

Student Organizations and Conferences

ASIAN PACIFIC AMERICAN MEDICAL STUDENT ASSOCIATION
(APAMSA; *https://www.apamsa.org/*)

APAMSA is a national organization of medical and premedical students committed to addressing the unique health challenges of Asian American, Native Hawaiian, and Pacific Islander (AANHPI) communities. It holds regional conferences and offers advocacy groups focused on the unique healthcare needs of the AANHPI community (such as the National APAMSA Hepatitis Conference).

EAST COAST ASIAN AMERICAN STUDENT UNION (ECAASU)– EAST COAST (*https://www.ecaasu.org/*)

Founded in 1989, ECAASU is a nonprofit dedicated to inspiring, educating, and empowering those engaged in AAPI matters. Led by volunteers, ECAASU conducts advocacy by reaching out to AAPI student organizations nationwide, educating individuals about driving change through its programs, most notably its annual conference.

INTERCOLLEGIATE TAIWANESE AMERICAN STUDENT ASSOCIATION (ITASA; *https://itasa.org/*)

Founded in 1993, ITASA links the Taiwanese American intercollegiate community, allowing emerging leaders to lead a nonprofit. Through programs and events, ITASA connects, inspires, and empowers students nationwide, fostering a network dedicated to Taiwan and Taiwanese American matters, while cultivating the next generation of leaders and collaborating with student organizations across the country.

MIDWEST ASIAN PACIFIC ISLANDER DESI AMERICAN STUDENTS UNION (MAASU; *https://www.maasu.org/*)

Founded in 1989, MAASU unites AAPI students in the Midwest (Colorado, Illinois, Indiana, Iowa, Kansas, Michigan, Minnesota, Missouri, Nebraska, Tennessee, Oklahoma, Ohio, and Wisconsin) to foster growth, leadership, activism, and communication. Its outreach extends to undergraduate, high school, and graduate students, empowering the APIDA community while collaborating annually with twenty colleges and universities.

NATIONAL ASIAN PACIFIC AMERICAN LAW STUDENT ASSOCIATION (NAPALSA; *https://www.napalsa.com/*)

Established in 1981, NAPALSA is the leading national organization for Asian Pacific American law students, committed to empowering them, fostering growth, and upholding community dignity. Through collaboration with legal and affinity groups, it is committed to inclusion and seeks to represent the diverse APA legal community.

ROBERT TOIGO FOUNDATION
(https://toigofoundation.org/)

Toigo focuses on enhancing institutions and individuals by promoting diversity and inclusion to strengthen organizations. Working with MBA programs and within the finance sector, Toigo strives to influence capital decisions and drive impactful solutions for inclusion and diversity in collaboration with leaders across various industries.

SPONSORS FOR EDUCATIONAL OPPORTUNITY
(SEO; *https://www.seo-usa.org/)*

Established in 1963, SEO is nonprofit organization dedicated to reducing academic and career disparities by bridging opportunity gaps for driven youth from historically marginalized communities. Annually, SEO's initiatives positively impact over seven thousand high school students, college students, and professionals nationwide through a variety of high-impact programs.

Media Resources

The following outlets are sources to get news and current information that are relevant to the Asian American community and the Asian diaspora. Their newsfeeds are not always covered by mainstream media.

THE JUGGERNAUT
(https://www.thejuggernaut.com/)

The Juggernaut is a media tech company and community that publishes well-reported stories about South Asia and South Asians. Publishing one news story each weekday, the platform covers everything from politics, culture, food, business, and technology. Its goal is to celebrate South Asian heritage but also challenge what the history books and community have gotten wrong.

NEXTSHARK
(*https://nextshark.com/*)

An online news and community, NextShark reports on business, culture, entertainment, politics, technology, and lifestyle from all over the world, with a focus on providing quality, up-to-date coverage for the Asian and Asian American community. NextShark's aim is to provide a platform to amplify and uplift Asian voices.

B

SEVEN STORIES
EXERCISE

Write down examples of ten to fifteen different experiences that meet the following criteria:

- You were good at it.

- You enjoyed it.

- You obtained a sense of accomplishment from it.

Feel free to draw upon a variety of past experiences, but make sure to **include at least two examples from work-related situations.** Try to pick a mix of experiences from every stage of your life (e.g., elementary school years, high school years, college years, early working years, most recent job).

Be specific (e.g., you were able to sell your senior leadership on a great new marketing idea; in high school you mobilized your classmates to design a life-size mural for your graduating class of three hundred; you received accolades at work because you managed the systems conversion effectively).

This is good:

"Completed a successful marketing project."

But this would be better:

"Convinced the senior leadership team to try out a marketing initiative that reached an untapped customer segment with potential for future revenues; led to an increase in market share."

1. _____

2. _____

3. _____

4. _____

5. _____

6. _____

7. _____

8. _____

9. _____

10. _____

11. _____

12. _____

13. _____

14. _____

15. _____

From your list of experiences, select seven that were the most important to you. Prioritize them from 1 through 7. For each, write down a short synopsis of the experience, using the following prompts.

STORY 1 ANALYSIS:

What role did you play in the story?

_____

What conditions allowed you to have a successful experience? What was the environment like?

_____

Who were the others involved in the story? Did you do it alone or with others?

_____

What made you good at what you did and what skills did you utilize?

_____

Complete a similar analysis of the next six stories.

BIBLIOGRAPHY

Asian Women United of California. *Making Waves: An Anthology of Writings by and about Asian American Women*. Boston: Beacon Press, 1989.

Australian Human Rights Commission. "Leading for Change: A Blueprint for Cultural Diversity and Inclusive Leadership Revisited." April 11, 2018. *https://humanrights.gov.au/our-work/race-discrimination/publications/leading-change-blueprint-cultural-diversity-and-0*.

Bell, Ella L. J., and Stella M. Nkomo. *Our Separate Ways: Black and White Women and the Struggle for Professional Identity*. Revised ed. Boston: Harvard Business Review Press, 2021.

Borchers, Callum. "Dear Co-workers: Call Me by My Real Name." *Wall Street Journal*, February 16, 2023. *https://tinyurl.com/WSJ-call-me-real-name*.

Budiman, Abby, and Neil G. Ruiz. "Key Facts about Asian Americans, a Diverse and Growing Population." Pew Research Center, April 29, 2021. *https://tinyurl.com/Key-Facts-Asian-Amer*.

Cadaval, Olivia. "How Cultural Resilience Made a Difference after Hurricane Hugo and Could Help Again." *Smithsonian Magazine*, October 3, 2017. *https://tinyurl.com/Cultural-Resilience-Hugo-Hugo*.

Chang, Kenneth. "Asian Researchers Face Disparity with Key U.S. Science Funding Source." *New York Times*, January 9, 2023. *https://www.nytimes.com/topic/organization/national-science-foundation*.

Chen, Christine Yifeng, Sara S. Kahanamoku, Aradhna Tripati, Rosanna A. Alegado, Vernon R. Morris, Karen Andrade, and Justin Hosbey. "Meta-Research: Systemic Racial Disparities in Funding Rates at the National Science Foundation." *eLife* 11 (2022): e83071. *https://doi.org/10.7554/eLife.83071*.

Chui, Michael, Kweilin Ellingrud, Ishanaa Rambachan, and Jackie Wong. "Asian American Workers: Diverse Outcomes and Hidden Challenges." McKinsey & Company, September 7, 2022, 7, 12. *https://tinyurl.com/McKinsey-outcomes-challenges*.

Clance, Pauline Rose, and Suzanne Ament Imes. "The Imposter Phenomenon in High Achieving Women: Dynamics and Therapeutic Intervention." *Psychotherapy: Theory, Research and Practice* 15, no. 3 (1978).

Cobbs, Price, and Judith Turnock. *Cracking the Corporate Code*. New York: Amacom Publishers, 2003.

Coffman, Julie, Bianca Bax, Alex Noether, and Brenen Blair. *The Fabric of Belonging: How to Weave an Inclusive Culture*. Boston: Bain & Company, 2022.

Conant, Douglas A. *The Blueprint: 6 Practical Steps to Raise Your Leadership to New Heights*. Hoboken, NJ: Wiley, 2020.

Conant, Douglas A., and Metter Norgaard, *Touchpoints*. San Francisco: Jossey-Bass, 2011.

Coqual. "The Power of Belonging: Why It Is and Why It Matters in Today's Workplace." Belonging Series, Part 1, June 22, 2020, 16, 17, 18. *https://coqual.org/reports/the-power-of-belonging/*.

Coqual. "Strangers at Home: The Asian and Asian American Professional Experience + The Erasure and Invisibility of Pacific Islander Professionals." January 19, 2023. *https://coqual.org/reports/strangers-at-home/*.

Csikszentmihalyi, Mihaly. *Flow: The Psychology of Optimal Experience*. New York: HarperPerennial, 1990.

Culture In The Workplace™ (CW). "Hofstede Culture in the Workplace Questionnaire." n.d. *https://www.cwqculture.com/*.

Daft, Richard L., and Robert H. Lengel. "Media Richness and Structural Design Theory." *Management Science* 32, no. 5 (May 1986): 554–71. *https://tinyurl.com/Media-Richness*

Dana, Deb. *Anchored: How to Befriend Your Nervous System Using Polyvagal Theory*. Louisville, CO: Sounds True Publishing, 2021.

Davidson, Martin N. *The End of Diversity as We Know It*. San Francisco: Berrett-Koehler, 2011.

De Mooij, Marieke K. *Global Marketing and Advertising: Understanding Cultural Paradoxes*. Thousand Oaks, CA: SAGE, 2022.

Dyer, Jeff, Hal Gregersen, and Clayton M. Christensen. *The Innovator's DNA: Mastering the Five Skills of Disruptive Innovators*. Boston: Harvard Business Review Press, 2011.

Ferrazzi, Keith, and Tahl Raz, *Never Eat Alone: And Other Secrets to Success, One Relationship at a Time*. Updated ed. New York: Crown Business, 2014.

Goldsmith, Marshall. *Triggers*. New York: Crown Business, 2015.

Goldsmith, Marshall. *What Got You Here Won't Get You There: How Successful People Become Even More Successful*. New York: Hachette Books, 2007.

Goss, Tracy. *The Last Word on Power: Executive Re-invention for Leaders Who Must Make the Impossible Happen*. New York: Crown Business, 1995.

Granovetter, Mark S. "The Strength of Weak Ties." *American Journal of Sociology* 78, no. 6 (1973): 1360–80.

Hall, Edward T. *The Silent Language*. New York: Anchor Books, 1973, 1990.

Hall, Edward T. *The Hidden Dimension*. New York: Anchor Books, 1990.

Hammer, Mitchell R. "Intercultural Development Inventory: A New Frontier in Assessment and Development of Intercultural Competence." In *Students Learning Abroad: What Our Students Are Learning, What They're Not, and What We Can Do about It*, edited by Michael Vande Berg, R. Michael Paige, and Kris Hemming Lou. Sterling, VA: Stylus, 2012.

Hammer, Mitchell R., Milton J. Bennett, and Richard Wiseman. "Measuring Intercultural Sensitivity: The Intercultural Development Inventory." *International Journal of Intercultural Relations* 27, no. 4 (2003): 421–43. *https://tinyurl.com/Intercultural -sensitivity*.

Harris, Carla A. *Expect to Win: 10 Proven Strategies for Thriving in the Workplace.* New York: Plume Books, 2009.

Heifetz, Ronald, Alexander Grashow, and Marty Linsky, *The Practice of Adaptive Leadership.* Boston: Harvard Business Press, 2009.

Hemmige, Harish, Rachel Ellison, and Allen Chen, "How Companies Can Bring More Asian Americans into the C-Suite." Boston Consulting Group, September 26, 2023. *https://www.bcg.com/publications/2023/how-companies-can-promote-asian -american-executives*.

Hewlett, Sylvia Ann, Ripa Rashid, Diana Forster, and Claire Ho. *Asians in America Unleashing the Potential of the "Model Minority."* New York: Center for Work-Life Policy, 2011.

Hofstede, Geert. "The 6-d Model of National Culture." n.d. *https://geerthofstede.com /culture-geert-hofstede-gert-jan-hofstede/6d-model-of-national-culture/*.

Hofstede, Geert, Gert Jan Hofstede, and Michael Minkov. *Culture and Organizations: Software of the Mind.* 3rd ed. New York: McGraw Hill Publishers, 2010.

Hyun, Jane. *Breaking the Bamboo Ceiling: Career Strategies for Asians.* New York: HarperCollins, 2005.

Hyun, Jane, and Audrey S. Lee. *Flex/The New Playbook for Managing across Differences.* New York: Harper Business, 2014, 26–30.

IMF Department of Asia and Pacific. "Opening Remarks and Presentation: IMF Press Briefing on Economic Outlook for Asia Pacific and Korea." Regional Economic Outlook for Asia and the Pacific, Incheon, Korea, May 3, 2023. *https://tinyurl.com /4kd46uy4*.

Joly, Hubert. "Legendary Retail CEO Hubert Joly's Playbook for Navigating the Culture Wars." *Fortune*, August 31, 2023. *https://tinyurl.com/Hubert-Jolys-Playbook*

Lane, Henry W., and Martha L. Maznevski. *International Management Behavior—Global and Sustainable Leadership.* Cambridge, UK: Cambridge University Press, 2019.

Lee, Thomas. "'Unapologetically Asian': Sneaker Startup Hopes to Project Pride and Cultural Power." *Boston Globe*, September 13, 2023. *https://tinyurl.com/1587-Sneakersz*

Lu, J. G. "A Creativity Stereotype Perspective on the Bamboo Ceiling: Low Perceived Creativity Explains the Underrepresentation of East Asian Leaders in the United States." *Journal of Applied Psychology*, advance online publication (2023). *https:// doi.org/10.1037/apl0001135*.

Mineo, Liz. "Good Genes Are Nice, but Joy Is Better." *Harvard Gazette*, April 11, 2017. *https://tinyurl.com/Genes-vs-Joy*.

Okazaki, Sumi, and Nancy Abelman. *Korean American Families in Immigrant America: How Teens and Parents Navigate Race.* New York: New York University Press, 2018.

Porges, Stephen W. "Polyvagal Theory." n.d. *https://www.stephenporges.com/*.

Racho, Maria Odiamar. "Attributes of Asian American Senior Leaders Who Have Retained Their Cultural Identity and Been Successful in American Corporations." *Theses and Dissertations* (2012): 290. *https://digitalcommons.pepperdine.edu/etd/290*.

Rajkumar, Karthik, Guillaume Saint-Jacques, Iavor Bojinov, Erik Brynjolfsson, and Sinan Aral. "A Causal Test of the Strength of Weak Ties." *Science* 377, no. 6612 (2022): 1304–10. *https://www.science.org/doi/10.1126/science.abl4476*.

Romo, Vanessa. "Very Few Architects Are Black. This Woman Is Pushing to Change That." NPR, March 12, 2023. *https://tinyurl.com/NPR-Diversity-in-Arch*.

Ruiz, Neil G., Luis Noe-Bustamante, and Sono Shah, "Diverse Cultures and Shared Experiences Shape Asian American Identities." Pew Research Center, May 8, 2023. *https://www.pewresearch.org/race-ethnicity/2023/05/08/diverse-cultures-and-shared-experiences-shape-asian-american-identities/*.

Sheffield, Daniel. *The Multicultural Leader: Developing a Catholic Personality*. 2nd ed. Jacksonville Beach, FL: Clements Publishing, 2015.

Shih, Howard, and Rimsha Khan. *Hidden in Plain Sight: Asian Poverty in the New York Metro Area*. New York: Asian American Federation, 2021. *https://tinyurl.com/AAF-Asian-PovertyNYC*.

Steele, Claude M. *Whistling Vivaldi: How Stereotypes Affect Us and What We Can Do*. New York: W. W. Norton & Company, 2010.

Thomas, David A. *Breaking Through: The Making of Minority Executives in Corporate America*. Boston: Harvard Business School Press, 1999.

Ting-Toomey, Stella. *Communicating across Cultures*. New York: Guilford Press, 1999.

Tokunaga, Paul. *Invitation to Lead: Guidance for Emerging Asian American Leaders*. Downers Grove, IL: Intervarsity Press, 2003.

Vande Berg, Michael R., Michael Paige, and Kris Hemming Lou, eds. *Students Learning Abroad: What Our Students Are Learning, What They're Not, and What We Can Do about It*. Sterling, VA: Stylus, 2012.

Van den Bosch, Ralph, and Toon Taris. "Authenticity at Work: Development and Validation of an Individual Authenticity Measure." *Journal of Happiness Studies* 15, no. 1 (2014). *https://tinyurl.com/Authenticity-at-work*

Wang, Jenny T. *Permission to Come Home: Reclaiming Mental Health as Asian Americans*. New York: Balance, 2022.

Webb, Caroline. *How to Have a Good Day*. New York: Currency Books, 2016.

Winters, Mary Frances. *We Can't Talk about That at Work! How to Talk about Race, Religion, Politics, and Other Polarizing Topics*. San Francisco: Berrett-Koehler, 2017.

Wolfe, Maren M., Peggy H. Yang, Eunice C. Wong, and Donald R. Atkinson. "Design and Development of the European American Values Scale for Asian Americans." *Cultural Diversity and Ethnic Minority Psychology* 7, no. 3 (2001): 274–83. *https://doi.org/10.1037/1099-9809.7.3.274*.

Wong, Ali. "Cathy Park Hong." 100 Most Influential People of 2021. *Time*, September 15, 2021. *https://time.com/collection/100-most-influential-people-2021/6096088/cathy -park-hong/*.

Yang, Allie. "After He Was Called a Slur on the Court, Jeremy Lin Highlights Surge in Anti-Asian Hate." ABC News, March 4, 2021. *https://tinyurl.com/hate-speech-on-court*.

Yoshino, Kenji. *Covering: The Hidden Assault on Our Civil Rights*. New York: Random House, 2006.

Yu, Corinna J., MD. "Asian Americans: The Overrepresented Minority?: Dispelling the 'Model Minority' Myth." *ASA Monitor*, July 2020. *http://tinyurl.com/AAPI -overrepresented-minority*.

Yun, Jessica. "The Bamboo Ceiling 2021: The 'Double Whammy' Asian Women Face in Their Careers." Yahoo Finance Australia, March 7, 2021. *https://tinyurl.com/4ytfcsjb*.

Zucker, Rebecca. "Managers Are Burned Out. Here's How to Help Them Recharge." *Harvard Business Review*, August 2, 2023. *https://tinyurl.com/Mgrs-Burned-Out-Help*.

ACKNOWLEDGMENTS

Our greatest fulfillment lies in giving ourselves to others.

—HENRI J. M. NOUWEN

Writing a book is a labor of love and a collective effort.

I didn't think anyone outside the Asian community would read my first book. I was wrong.

I'm grateful to every individual who has reached out to me by email, LinkedIn, or at a book signing since *Breaking the Bamboo Ceiling* was released and opened up their hearts to the book and to exploring what it means to be Asian American in the workplace. From first-time managers to CEOs, they asked me tough questions I didn't have easy answers to and entrusted me with their most painful moments of defeat and personal triumphs, which were the impetus behind my writing this book. They weren't all Asian, either. I was overwhelmed by friends from different cultural, ethnic, and racial communities around the world who reached out because they saw themselves as cultural "outliers" and told me that the book helped them too.

I couldn't do my consulting, speaking, and coaching work without my incredible colleagues. Betsyann, Andrew, Norm, Andy, Alison, Miguel, and Lisa—you are true experts in your craft and I'm deeply grateful for your partnership. Kudos to the CEOs, ERG leads and sponsors, and Chief Diversity officers who saw the value of their Asian American workforce enough to take action, and entrusted us to build their leadership capability and learn with them.

The team at Berrett-Koehler: my editor, Lesley Iura, for her guidance; art director Ashley Ingram for her calm, fair hand in helping me land on a cover design; Maureen Forys and Rachel Monaghan for spearheading the production process with grace (you gave me the keys to the kingdom with the magic of H1 and H2). Christy Kirk and Kristen Frantz, and Steve Piersanti, who persistently pursued me for eight years to join their community.

Thanks to Jiani Xiao at Agenda for this beautiful cover design. Daniel Koh, you're my hero! I'm grateful to you both for your artistry and professionalism.

Many thanks to B. G. Dilworth, a great advocate and astute sounding board who articulates the heart of any issue.

I learned so much from the many people who've come into my life through learning sessions and speaking engagements. So, I thank all of those students of this work *who taught me* this book was absolutely needed and wanted.

The village included many talented and insightful individuals. I want to acknowledge the steady hand of Rachel Carter to shape my ideas and thoughts, Peter Gutierrez for his surgical precision when I hit a fork in the road, and Betsyann Faiella for her careful shaping of my thoughts and just being there when I felt stuck and had to come up with words that reflected what I was feeling. Joan Smoller came to my rescue during critical junctures of my brainstorming process and was a constant cheerleader. Thanks to Mathea Li Olson and Betsyann for pulling the list of Asian professional organizations together!

Anne Marie Yarwood and Comet were my constant companions during our evening walks. Who could forget eating Thai food while marking up my book outline together?! I still have the stains from the chicken kra pow on that first draft. Rhonda McLean was my beacon of light. Her book, *Black Women of Influence*, written with Marsha Haygood and Elaine Meryl Brown, is a constant inspiration.

Ella Bell and Stella Nkomo, I will cherish my life-giving weekend of being mentored by you both in Vermont. Thank you.

Every year I get to work with fifteen to eighteen MBA students at Columbia. They bring unabashed enthusiasm and humility to the practice of leadership—I love every minute we get to work together! My exec ed class at the

NAMIC ELDP program at Darden is an annual reminder that when you bring top multicultural talent together, you're incubating excellence and lifelong friendships. Your leadership inspires me, Martin Davidson.

A number of people dedicated time, insights, and brainpower to this project: Iyleen Summer, Michael Gonzales, Ivan Lee, Sue Yim, Moon Sung, Elaine Cha, Gwen Houston, Dan Sheffield, Shelley Dinehart, Djuana Beamon, Ashley Modisett, and others held me accountable. Your heart for this book and your willingness to provide feedback showed me how much you cared. You were my lifeline during those late nights.

For opening their hearts to share their personal stories with me: Alena Brown, Marshall Cho, Anand Chokkalingam, Kim Cummings, Naava Frank, Michael Gonzales, Ben Hires, Veena Lakkundi, Jenny Lee, Bryan MacDonald, David Moore, David Nguyen, Preeti Sriratana, Mino Tsumura, Marie Segura, Hollee McGinnis, and Grace Chiang Nicolette.

Thomas Windsor, James Cheng, Jim Jones, Liana Loh, Ha-Young Woo, and Keysha Hall always provided perspective and wisdom when I needed it.

The Friends of Hofstede community: Cass and John Bing, Silvania Chadú, David de Jong, Cindy Gong, Angelika Groterath, Miguel Gurrola, Claudia Harss, Roberto Hernández, Gert Jan Hofstede, Loes Hosain-Cornelissen, Thomas Imfeld, Lea Kirchmann, Fernando Lanzer, Jin Lee Teo, Romie Littrell, Kirsty MacEachen, Angelina Mah, Benjamin Mao, Stephen Martin, Chika Miyamori, Denise Pang, Kavita Sethi, Lara Potma, Charlotte Paetzold, Sjaak Pappe, Christina Roettgers, Itzel Ruiz, Nav Singh, Candida Snow, Ralf van Haastregt, Anne van Marsenille, Gert Jan van Reenen, Huib Wursten, and others. . . . The visual memory of being in the "same boat" with you is emblazoned in my memory.

Sincere gratitude to Mary-Frances Winters for her encouragement and challenging me to get my work out there. I remember you approaching me in 2005 after a speaking event and enthusiastically showing interest in my work. Mareisha Reese, you inspire me with your enthusiasm and vision.

I was fortunate enough to meet my author B-K community early—Massimo Bachus, Joe Davis, and Fatimah Gilliam, I can't wait to see your books come to life.

Thanks to the board members of NAAAP (Ron, D. A., Michael, Fabian, Kim, Mo, Liz, Aurora, Ashley, Shim) and the local chapters for your devotion to the Asian American community.

Serving at Exodus alongside Lisa Ortiz, Geoff Davenport, David Turley, Phil Lee, Chris Mowery-Bell, Nate Meeks, Rosina Roa, Jim McKinney, Lana Kim, and working with the Exodus team of Mark Gonzales, Julissa Lopez, Kim Collado, Natalie Muñoz, and Esther Acosta, has taught me a lot about community. Walking and working with you all has been an absolute privilege.

I'm grateful to Mitch Hammer and the team at IDI—Lea, Diann, and Neil Hammer, Ryon Downing, Diane Washington, Mercedes Reaves, Tracy Tachiera, and Emily Aiken—for their heartfelt support.

And my fellow IDI faculty and moderators: Mafalda Arias, Phyllis Braxton, Julius Erolin, Deb Freathy, Hamlin Grange, Terrence Harewood, Tara Harvey, Mylon Kirksy, Akiko Maeker, Amy Moreno-Sherwood, Joann Reeck, Blaire Tinker, Nehrwr Reuel, Beth Zemsky, and Allison Smith-Steffenhagen. I'm blessed with the extraordinary honor of facilitating with an insightful group of interculturalists.

We lost Michael Paige too soon. Facilitating the Philly seminars with you meant so much to me. Your quick laugh, intercultural wit, and willingness to try *any* new foods will be remembered.

There are those who remind you of your calling when you have no energy left. Deepest gratitude to Doug Conant, Pete Bye, Fiona Wong, David Shriner-Cahn, Gary Ireland, Naava Frank, Joan Smoller, Greg Jenkins, Linda Kelly, Deb Dagit, and Donna Fullerton for your guidance and lifegiving advice.

Thank you, Ted Childs, for your pioneering work.

To Erby Foster, a champion and advocate for our Cultural Fluency in Leadership Academy, whose life was cut too short.

Elaine Cha, Moon Sung, Sujin Chang, and Carolyn Oh, my beloved superpowers who root for me behind the scenes.

To Kyung Yoon and So-Chung Shinn-Lee, for being there when I have questions that no one else could answer.

David, you always put us first and love us deeply. Abigail and Tim, thanks for accepting me with all my quirks. You inspire me to be better than yesterday! You gave me space to hole myself up in my room to write without complaining.

To my parents and Susan, my dear sister, who told me I could be anything and always supported me in that idea. I miss you, Umma and Appa, and I feel your prayers in my heart every day.

To mom (Jewel), I'm grateful for your ever-present love and encouragement. Your presence is missed every day, Dad (Chul Woo Hyun). Alyce, Rob, Lowell, and Josephine, thank you for your support.

For many years, Price Cobbs encouraged me to write a follow-up to my first book to share the lessons learned from our work together with the leaders at PepsiCo and other Fortune 500 companies. I hope he'd be proud of this contribution.

INDEX

ABOUT THE AUTHOR

Often called an "interpreter," **JANE HYUN** is a global leadership strategist who has collaborated with corporate clients across five continents. She has dedicated her life to guiding leaders to bring their full selves to the workplace through her Cultural Fluency Academy and to closing the Asian leadership gap inside Fortune 500 companies. Jane speaks on the topics of culture, effective teams, and adaptive leadership. The bestselling author of *Breaking the Bamboo Ceiling* and coauthor of *Flex: The New Playbook for Managing across Differences*, Jane has appeared on CNN, CNBC, and NPR; has been featured in the *Washington Post*, *Economist*, and *Atlantic*; and has written for the *Harvard Business Review*, *Fast Company*, and *Forbes*. She is a recipient of the Marshall Goldsmith Global Coaches Award as the #1 coach for cultural fluency. A graduate of Cornell University, she lives in New York City.

www.leadershiptoolkitforasians.com

Dear reader,

Thank you for picking up this book and welcome to the worldwide BK community! You're joining a special group of people who have come together to create positive change in their lives, organizations, and communities.

What's BK all about?

Our mission is to connect people and ideas to create a world that works for all.

Why? Our communities, organizations, and lives get bogged down by old paradigms of self-interest, exclusion, hierarchy, and privilege. But we believe that can change. That's why we seek the leading experts on these challenges—and share their action-able ideas with you.

A welcome gift

To help you get started, we'd like to offer you a **free copy** of one of our best-selling ebooks:

www.bkconnection.com/welcome

When you claim your **free ebook**, you'll also be subscribed to our blog.

Our freshest insights

Access the best new tools and ideas for leaders at all levels on our blog at ideas. bkconnection.com.

Sincerely,

Your friends at Berrett-Koehler

Certified

Corporation